Sanity after Seventy

Sage and Sassy Reflections
on the Golden Years
… by a woman who is living them

By

Betty J. Durden

Sanity after Seventy

Sage and Sassy Reflections
on the Golden Years
… by a woman who is living them

Renaissance Aviation Publishing
Colorado

ISBN 978-0-9834222-2-8
PRINTED IN THE UNITED STATES OF AMERICA

Lines From the Edge

This little volume is lovingly dedicated to my children, Richard, David, and Barbara, and to my grandchildren, Scott, Laura, Amelia, Erin, and Erika. It is intended to give a view of my life over the years and a glimpse of my present life in this, my last Community.

Betty Dillavou Durden

(Mrs. Jesse N. Durden, Jr.)

Foreword

Betty Durden's writings are a delightful look at life in the very mature years. Her contemporaries and their families find her writing perceptive, astute, and filled with compassion. They show her to be a constant observer of nature, feeling herself a part of the natural world, and a believer in the connectedness of all things.

Readers enjoy Betty's occasionally caustic remarks and her impatience with superficial "niceness." They appreciate her encouragement to be open to change, honest with themselves and others, and grateful for life.

As a person who has worked many years with older people, I am well acquainted with their needs. I encourage anyone in their later years, as well as those who will soon be entering them, to sample Betty's clear and helpful messages. They would enjoy a peek into the world of aging. It will bring them surprise, hope, and inspiration.

Betty Grandquist, Retired Director

Iowa Department of Elder Affairs

TABLE OF CONTENTS

Prayer of Invocation

Eternally gracious God,

Giver of every good and perfect gift,

Grant to us now that gift our hearts most desire:

The gift of Your presence.

Let words here spoken

Become to us Your Word of Life.

Let prayers said become the full and honest outpouring
of our hearts.

Let our expressions of love for You,

For one another, and for Your world

Become the foundation

Of a commitment to lives of joyful service.

Help us to make honest and honorable choices

In these troubled times.

Support us as we try to discern Your message

Of hope and love for all humankind.

Amen.

FIRST THOUGHTS

A Dark View

In my ongoing effort to be clear and transparent, I shall reveal certain things about myself. As you know, "transparent" now means, "I'm telling you everything. What are you hiding?" This is a term much used by people running for office and others of ill repute.

I am not now, nor ever have been, an insider. I am an observer. Few people really like observers.

Personally, I like people more when they are working than when they are playing. When they are working very hard at having fun at a party, I don't like them at all.

People who say they just love people are kidding me or themselves.

I have no patience with people who are convinced their political or religious views are beyond question and I must share them.

People who want others to fix problems their own actions caused irritate me.

People who think their children never do anything wrong need a reality check. This does not apply to my children or grandchildren.

Many people hear what they want to and make up the rest.

Unless you are Rose Kennedy, please do not tell me about your children or grandchildren when I'm trying to tell you about mine.

Another thing about foreigners: if they would only try harder, they could speak English. This is the U.S. of A. and they should speak our official language. I don't like it when they talk to each other in some strange language. They are talking about me, and I want it to stop.

I'm glad your husband liked your hairdo. How long has he been gone?

I don't want to talk about religion or politics unless you agree with me.

My clothes are getting a little tight, but you are getting fat. It's all those desserts the food servers force us to order.

Why are men considered so fortunate to eat dinner with several "ladies"? We "ladies" have eaten a lot of meals with men, and they weren't such good company.

Life is a huge jigsaw puzzle without a picture to follow. We're all struggling to fit in the pieces and come out even.

Notes and Comments

Perhaps it is time that I include some credentials, to make myself more or possibly less qualified to write these thoughts. After WWII, I graduated with a B.A. from Drake University, as an English major. The G.I. Bill paid for much of this schooling, and my husband was supportive of my educational goals. After many years of sitting on hard chairs in various classrooms, I now hold a Doctorate in Education (Ed.D.) with emphasis on counseling and personnel services. In addition, I have a lifetime certificate as a Senior Professional in Human Resources.

I like to plan, organize, implement, set goals, and achieve them. For nearly twenty years, I was an administrator at Drake University. I can develop and manage a budget, although I prefer words to numbers. I don't really know how to teach anyone how to think or to write. Much as I have studied people, they continue to amaze me.

I am not a sentimental person. I have been told that I think like a man. This was intended to be a compliment. I am ambivalent about that. I don't think brains come gender-coded. I have worked more with men than women and have found that oftentimes, neither gender thinks at all.

Most people think I am an extrovert. I really prefer to bury myself deep inside a chambered nautilus, peering out but protected from involvement with others. Some people have cared for me very much. That's all I need.

A deep strain of skepticism keeps me from achieving my desired level of religious belief. A voice inside keeps warning me, "It ain't necessarily so." I do not believe in coincidence, chance, fate, or a Divinity-designed master plan for my life. I believe in marriage before children, obviously an old-fashioned belief. I believe in both goodness and evil and strive toward the former. I am convinced of human brilliance and stupidity. I also believe in free will, the chaos theory, showing up, and personal responsibility, and that there are other worlds and populations we cannot even imagine. The greatest gift to humans is intelligence. Most religions seek knowledge. I'll go with that. I feel privileged to have experienced life, but don't want to do it again. Mostly, it has been good.

One of the women at dinner recently referred to some residents as "the swells." I tried to think whom she meant. It was clear that she didn't mean me. I still don't know—nor does it matter. There are widely different financial levels represented here, but basically we're all in this together. Some days are better than others, but not some residents. Equality without pretense seems to suit us best at this stage of our lives.

A dear friend of mine has moved from Des Moines to a retirement facility in Grinnell. She called after my last visit there and wanted to plan another meeting. "If we both start driving, we could meet in Newton," she said. It sounded so reasonable, but she has not driven in several years. A concerned daughter took her keys and later sold her car. I will continue to visit her in Grinnell as long as I can drive or ride with others. Minds should not leave us while our bodies are still alive.

My goal in these little scribblings is to speak the truth with love, humor, and compassion, and maybe touch a few nerves.

FAMILY

Iowa Stubborn

As early as I can remember, I had two homes. One home was on an Iowa farm where there were various adults, cows, horses, sheep, cats, a shepherd dog, and one small child — me. At two years of age, my world consisted of my elderly parents, who were then forty-two and forty-four. My siblings were a brother, seventeen; a sister, nineteen; and a brother known only from his pictures and letters. He was twenty-one and a graduate of the U.S. Naval Academy.

The animals were my playmates, my dolls were my real family, and my dog was my security blanket and defender. Everyone and everything in my world revolved around me and existed for my care and comfort.

At various times, other adults lived with us and added to my pleasure or intruded on my privacy. Grandpa Otis, my mother's father, lived with us. My grandmother had died years before I was born, so had no reality for me. Grandpa was a big, white-haired man who was incredibly old and useless as far as contributing to the work of the farm. He could gather the eggs and find where the hens had hidden them in inconvenient and therefore safe corners of the barn or henhouse. He often took me along on these treasure hunts, showing me how to lift the old biddy off her nest without getting pecked in the process. It was work that needed to be done daily, and the eggs added to our food supplies and meager cash income, but it was women's work. Grandfather's years of earning his keep were over, and mine had not yet begun.

Grandpa Otis died when I was fourteen years old, in high school, and I mourned him, not so much as a person but as someone who had populated my world and was gone. I remembered his hard fingers when he thumped me for some mischief I had done and missed holding his big, strong hand when we searched for eggs in the scary, shadowy corners of the barn.

My Uncle Joe, Mother's brother, lived with us from time to time, between sessions of drinking which left him ill and homeless. He stayed in one of our five upstairs bedrooms and recovered sufficiently to be an unpaid hired man. Dad directed the outdoor labors by pointing out a machine or barn or field and expecting the helper to know what to do and go do it. Most of the workers would have benefited from more specific directions, but they were not provided. Dad believed that if the hired man was not lazy or ignorant, the necessary labors would be obvious to him. Continual disappointments in the results of this type of supervision, or lack of it, never changed his method. He was just more convinced that most hired men were both lazy and stupid. That was probably why they did not have their own farms to run and enjoy as he did.

Uncle Joe was the most entertaining of the adults in my world, much to Mother's dismay. She was in total agreement with the women who took axes to bars and knew that all drinkers and purveyors of hard drink were headed straight to eternal punishment. She was very fond of her wayward older brother with his quick wit and cheerful disregard of proper behavior, but she did not expect to share eternity with him.

Father also had a family member who was an occasional part of our household. Aunt Goldie gave willingly of her homemaking skills in exchange for a safe place to stay while her shiftless husband was otherwise occupied. This was never explained to me. Her cinnamon rolls could entice the sleepiest youngster or tired hired hand out of bed. The delicious smell of fresh rolls still reminds me of Goldie, but I can't remember how she looked or dressed. I accepted her presence in an upstairs bedroom or at the stove in the big, inconvenient kitchen but when she was gone, there was no feeling of loss. Why she came and why she left did not concern me, and such things were not discussed where little ears could hear. Mother was grateful for her help with the cooking and washing chores, and no one resented her presence or commented on her return to whatever home she had. Father accepted his role of provider as part of his preordained duty as a country man. There was plenty of work to be done, and more hands were welcome.

Goldie may have had children of her own, but they didn't come with her to our house. People had children or they didn't. It made very little difference to me. My brothers and sister were interesting, but not essential to my daily activities. It was years later when I learned from my mother why there was such a gap between my brother and me. Seven miscarriages in those years accounted for our age difference and contributed to my mother's ailments.

I asked Mother, when I dared, if she had wanted another baby when she was so old. She said, "Betty Jean, I didn't want just another baby. I wanted you." We never talked about this again.

We agreed that I must have hung on tight to survive the months in her frail body and live when the others had not. It was then that I decided that I was stubborn even before birth and probably always would be.

Mother, Father, and a succession of hired girls from the state training school filled my world with love, discipline, and continuity. Each deserves a chapter in a future autobiography and so they shall have. The second home will be described later.

Springing Forward

I have just begun a new part of the year, and so have you. It isn't New Years, or the Summer Solstice, or any defined and expected transition from one season to another. It occurs when we follow instructions (whose?) and set our clocks one hour ahead on Saturday night. On Sunday morning, we awaken to a subtle difference in the morning light. Unfortunately, there was no morning light on this rainy morning. The only difference I noticed was a reluctance to leave my bed an hour early.

The end to my night's sleep interrupted a very unpleasant dream. I have read many interpretations of dreams, none of them very satisfactory. I don't know for sure what my dreams mean, and I am content with not knowing. At my age, I can write my own meaning into my experiences, both awake and asleep. I doubt that Dr. Jung will arise from his grave and tell me I'm wrong. I think that dreams do have meaning but, like many other things in life, there are no absolutes. Sometimes I long for absolutes, but there are few to be found. I can live with that.

As I left my bed and stumbled to the bathroom, threads of my dream followed me, connecting me to a different world, one of anxiety and danger. What was troubling me, my children would ask, if I revealed my disturbed night and continuing unease upon awakening. I would tell them I had no idea. But I did. One of my granddaughters, a beautiful girl newly turned seventeen, is struggling to find her way to responsible adulthood. She is hurtling down a train track with wrong signals and dangerous crossings.

The runaway train I had seen in my dream was carrying its passengers toward a deadly collision. My frantic attempt to stop it was interrupted by my alarm clock, but my anxiety lingered. How would this image have ended? It haunts me. How do we prevent the disasters we can foresee? Sometimes we can't.

Does every generation have to find its own way, make its own mistakes? What good are all our years of experience if we can't share them and prevent our loved ones from suffering? This is another of life's mysteries, but I won't stop trying. How can I make her hear me?

God of Us All

We come to You with faith and doubt,

Humility and arrogance,

Courage and fear,

Joy and sorrow —

All of our strengths and weaknesses we bring to You. We ask Your blessing on us as we are and on the persons we are struggling to become.

We come to You singly in silence and surrounded by others who share our journey to faith and acceptance and love.

Help us to be silent and hear Your voice, be quiet, and allow Your presence to fill our being, speak with love and caring as You have taught us, work with us as we work, rest with us as we rest. Loving God, help us to be open to Your eternal truths and love.

We are here to feel and receive Your presence with us, among us and in us.

We turn ourselves to Your light, pray for Your guidance in our lives, and strive to remain open to new spiritual possibilities.

Free us, guide us, strengthen us, help us to grow in the direction You would have us go.

Thank You. We are grateful for Your world and for Your eternal love.

Amen.

WORLD WAR II

Memories

What do you remember about World War II? That is a question that a committee I'm on is asking as we design a lifelong learning class on the Great War. This question has brought up many memories of that period of my life. I'd like to share some of them with you.

I graduated from high school in 1940 when barely seventeen. That fall I went away to college, sixty-five miles from my farm home south of Jefferson in Greene County. Drake University was acceptable to my parents because it was founded by the Christian Church (Disciples of Christ) and because I could live with my sister and her husband at 41st and College Streets on the University trolley line. It also helped that Drake had awarded me a small but useful scholarship. My life appeared to be on a predictable course.

To the surprise of my parents and friends, I decided not to return to college the following fall in 1941. The courses were challenging and I was a successful and diligent student, but I wanted to learn more about the world and myself. I also wanted to earn some money and establish my independence. I was eighteen years old.

So far as I can remember, I had no idea what was going on in the world and how these events would impact me and redefine my future.

I looked for a job in Des Moines trying to market my typing and shorthand skills learned in high school.

To my amazement, no one wanted to hire me. Finally, I heard that the Federal Bureau of Investigation was hiring for clerical positions in Washington, D.C. I filled out the paperwork and submitted to an in-depth scrutiny of my activities, which were not extensive or even very interesting. A Special Agent visited my little home community, asking questions about my family and me. Neighbors were questioned. People who knew me only as the little Dillavou girl had a visit from a real FBI agent. I was only applying to be a typist! Evidently, I passed the inspection because I received a job offer. The pay, as I remember, was $120 a month. I was thrilled. My parents were not.

I can only imagine the discussions my mother and dad had about letting their youngest child go to Washington, D.C., alone to live and work in a strange and probably dangerous city. What would you have done?

What they did was give me their blessing and let me go. My older sister drove the four of us to Washington, more than a thousand miles away. They stayed until I was settled in a "women's club," really just a boarding house for some of the hundreds of women who worked in the offices of the U.S. government.

I was not the first of my parents' four children to seek a different life from the one they knew. My oldest brother, who was nineteen when I was born, was appointed to the U.S. Naval Academy when he graduated first in his high school class. How could this farm couple imagine what his life would be as a career naval officer? I'm sure they knew he would never return to stay. They wanted the best for their children. It must have been wrenching to let him go, but they did.

When I went to Washington in August 1941, he was a Lt. Commander in the Navy and stationed at Pearl Harbor. The attack on December 7, 1941, changed all of our lives. My brother did survive, but we didn't know for four days if he was alive or dead.

I worked at the FBI headquarters in Washington for a year and a half until I had earned enough money to pay for tuition, board, room, and books in college in Iowa. While in Washington, I met a young man from Georgia who worked in the Fingerprint Department of the Bureau. He could have been deferred, but he joined the Naval Air Corps as a cadet.

As soon as I was old enough, I joined the WAVES. By this time, my brother was a Captain in the Navy. I was an Apprentice Seaman, the lowest enlisted rate in the Navy. We were proud of each other.

The Navy Air Corps cadet and I were married at the Naval Air Training Bases in Pensacola, Florida, the day he got his wings and became an Ensign. He stayed there as an instructor and I was discharged from the WAVES a few months later.

At about the time we were married, my sister learned that her Army captain husband had died in England. He was a physician just starting his practice in Des Moines. He was too old to be drafted, but he voluntarily joined the Army because doctors were needed. Their only child was two years old when he was sent overseas and four when he died. My sister raised their son alone.

My husband and I chose to settle in Iowa and never regretted our decision. We both used the G.I. Bill for college expenses. That bill that allowed veterans to further their education was one of the greatest agents of social change ever established.

Where were you when you heard that Pearl Harbor had been attacked? I'm sure you remember. Our world was forever changed.

WAVES, World War II

I feel unworthy to present myself as a veteran before you men who went through such horrendous experiences in the service during WW II. How did you survive? Your strength of character, faith, courage, and luck pulled you through. We all honor you and the many others who did not come home.

I was a student at the University of Iowa when I enlisted in the WAVES in 1944. After a year at Drake University, I "stopped out" to work in Washington, D.C., to make some money and learn to be on my own. When I had earned enough to pay for tuition and living expenses, I returned to Iowa to attend the University of Iowa where the tuition was manageable.

There were many women on campus, but few civilian men. The men in uniform were in the Army Corps of Engineers or were Navy Preflight cadets. The Navy cadets were available to date because they were not supposed to be married, but the Army engineers were older and probably married. I worked as a student in the Engineering College office, for 45 cents an hour, so I met many of the engineers. A sympathetic secretary would find out if a particular Army man was married or single, if I considered dating him.

Campus life felt increasingly removed from the real world. I felt that I was not contributing to the war effort and wanted to do my part. Women did not have to be in the military, and most women were not, but I wanted to be in the Navy.

My oldest brother, nineteen years old when I was born, had been appointed to the U.S. Naval Academy upon graduation from Jefferson High School in Iowa. He had been at Annapolis two years when I arrived. My family was always very proud of our Navy man, as I was also.

Years later, as a Lt. Commander, he was stationed at Pearl Harbor when it was attacked. My parents did not know for several days whether or not he had survived. Fortunately, he did and continued his Navy career in various posts until his retirement.

◆ ◆ ◆

A number of my high school classmates, Iowa boys still in their teens, had joined the Iowa National Guard to make some spending money, never expecting to see wartime service. They were called up very early in the war and sent to North Africa to fight Rommel's troops. Some later returned. Some were captured and sent to Germany as prisoners of war. Some never came home.

Their involvement in the fighting made a huge impact on me. The war became very real and personal. These were my friends, boys I had grown up with. They were risking their lives. What was I doing?

I enlisted in the WAVES in 1944 when I was old enough to join without my parents' signatures. Being young and naïve, I thought the Navy would welcome me. The woman officer who interviewed me said,

"What makes you think you have anything to offer the Navy?" If she was trying to discourage me, her words had the opposite effect. Actually, I thought about that question many times later, but that was after I had signed my freedom away.

My family was not impressed with my decision. My brother, the Navy man I wanted to be proud of me, was not either. My boyfriend, later to be my husband, was a Navy flight cadet when I enlisted. He was appalled. He was aware of the WAVES who were mechanics and worked on the flight line. He thought that if I was assigned to that job, the whole Air Force was in jeopardy.

Well, so much for auspicious beginnings. I was sent to Hunter College in New York for orientation and training. There I lived with eleven other women in an apartment with one bathroom and started to learn how to do things the Navy way. I found I really enjoyed marching, feeling a part of a team, following commands, keeping the lines straight, looking sharp. One woman who seemed to have two left feet was sent home, and I felt sorry for her.

Our uniforms were wonderful. Never have I felt so perfectly dressed as I did in my Navy blues and the dress whites; not so much in the seersucker uniform, which I appreciated later in the Florida heat. After I learned to tie the tie and put my hat squarely on my head, I felt very comfortable and proud in my uniform.

I liked my roommates. We kept our sparsely furnished apartment ready for inspection at all times. They really did do white glove inspections. I found the Navy food filling and too abundant. Civilians were rationed on meat and other items, but we were overfed.

My family became accustomed to their Navy daughter and somewhat pleased with her growing independence. My Navy brother, now a Captain—you know, the four gold stripes on the sleeve and "scrambled eggs" on the cap—visited me at Hunter College. I was still an Apprentice Seaman, and there is nothing lower in the Navy. When I hugged the Captain, I could hear the gasp from everyone in the room.

After boot camp, the placement people sent me back to Iowa, to the Teachers College (now Northern Iowa University) in Cedar Falls for yeoman training. I was still surprised that I had survived boot camp. I had enjoyed much of it, the classes on naval history, and most of the other subjects they force-fed us. Well, not the lectures on VD and other diseases I had never heard of.

From yeoman school, I was sent to my permanent duty station, the personnel office on Mainside at the Naval Air Training Bases at Pensacola, Florida. There I was assigned to report to a Chief Yeoman, as were the other yeomen in the office. He had many hashmarks on his sleeve, none for good conduct, as I remember. His opinion of women was predictable. Women had their place, but it was not in the Navy. Actually, we learned a lot from him, including some additions to our vocabularies.

There were five of us female yeomen in the office, along with two male yeomen first class. If you think the men were pleased to have women come to relieve them so they could go to overseas duty, you were very mistaken. They were courteous to us, but mostly ignored us.

The Chief gradually accepted our presence, but reluctantly, and never thought we should be considered a part of *his* Navy. The ultimate irony was that he later married one of us, a short, dark-haired Cajun woman from Baton Rouge. I'm sure she managed him well.

My husband-to-be was also at the Naval Air Training Bases in Pensacola, completing his flight training, having survived the fifty-percent washout rate. We were married the day he received his wings and his commission, May 5, 1945. His friends said he got his wings in the morning and got them clipped in the afternoon. Our Navy friends attended our brief ceremony in the Navy chapel, but our families could not come.

We expected my husband to be sent to the Pacific theater. Instead, he was given orders to stay on at Pensacola at Corry Field as an instructor, a new ensign giving retraining to returning lieutenants and higher officers. We lived in various rooms "ashore" because we were not eligible for quarters on the base. Enlisted don't live with officers, even if they're married.

I was discharged in late 1945, and he was released to inactive duty in 1946 but stayed in the reserves. Although he had been born in Georgia, we left the South without regrets and settled in Des Moines, Iowa, where we raised our three children.

◆ ◆ ◆

The G.I. Bill was very helpful as we completed our educations. I finally graduated from Drake University and in many ways never left. I shall always be grateful for my Navy service. I wish other young people could experience the "coming of age" opportunities that the Navy provided me.

Alzheimer's disease stole my husband's memory. Those of us who are here remember and speak for those who are no longer here. It is a privilege to be with you.

Eternally Gracious God

We have gathered to affirm the greatest truths we know: that Your love is the foundation of our lives, and loves, and labors; that worship is the most important thing we can do to become more fully Your people.

Bless our gathering with Your presence, that we might find here comfort and challenge, peace and power; then send us forth to live as we believe.

Amen.

BLESSINGS

A Sudden Startling Joy

Those words were spoken by a friend recently. I have recited and savored them since she said them. I don't know what she meant or why she spoke as she did, but I am grateful to her for their explosive joy.

What brings us a burst of joy? This is my list. What is yours?

Waking up refreshed from a good night's sleep.

Watching the ground fog recede and the trees gradually appear out of the mist.

Seeing an egret extend its long neck to catch food as it stands gracefully on the riverbank.

Feeling a kinship with an old bare tree standing straight and dignified among younger trees. Devoid of adornment, we're still standing.

Coming over a rise and seeing wind generators appear in the distance, first one and gradually all seven, their huge blades turning purposefully, capturing energy. I see my father turning on our windmill to charge the Delco battery, which gave us electricity and made our lives more comfortable. What will power our grandchildren's lives?

Finding Joy

Holy Reading and Holy Listening

Last month at the first vesper service, we brought a message about the goodness of creation and of the world in which we live. This message was taken from the beautiful story from Genesis of God's creation of the universe. It does not matter whether this story is literal truth to you, or whether it is a poetic description of the beginning of the complex universe that we cannot fully comprehend. What matters is that we are a part of this mystery, and we believe in its ultimate goodness and our contribution to that goodness.

In these few weeks from the first vesper service to tonight, terrible events have occurred. We have been reminded of the assassination of the Reverend Martin Luther King, Jr. We have watched and listened to the accounts of the horrible slayings and woundings in Tucson. Closer to home, we have experienced the loss of some dear friends and family members here. We feel overwhelmed, fearful, sad, and helpless. How can we say that the world is good when we know of the evil that exists in it?

Tonight we have the audacity to say to you that we can experience joy in the midst of sorrow and pain. Tonight we come together in community to share in the art of holy reading and holy listening. We share familiar words and music. We share the pleasure of eating together on an otherwise lonely Sunday evening. We share the view of the darkening sky outside these windows and know that we are safe within. We share the bonds of fellowship and community. We talk together and then we become silent to listen to holy words and uplifting music. We reverently pray together.

As we speak and listen in this short service, our thoughts turn inward and fly upward. Our breathing slows, our movements grow less agitated and then relax into rest. A Sabbath calm surrounds and enfolds us.

Yes, there is evil, sadness, and fear in the world. Those of us gathered here have known life's trials and personal tragedies. We are here among friends, caring for ourselves and lending our hands and hearts to those around us. Our loved ones are an eternal part of our lives, even though many are no longer with us. God has granted us these years on earth, and we are living them well. Now is the time to seek peace and joy by forgiving ourselves and others, by achieving reconciliation. Our bodies may no longer find healing, but that which is eternal remains strong within us.

It is possible, indeed necessary and honest, to say that creation is good and we are a significant part of it. We are more than a tiny speck in this vast universe. Now is a time to be grateful for life, to find joy in this life and comfort in the promise of the life to come.

It Is Good

And God saw everything that He had made,
And behold, it was very good.
Genesis 1:31

Our willingness to rest depends on what we believe
we will find there. At rest, we come face to face with
the essence of life. If we believe life is fundamentally
good, we will seek out rest as a taste of that goodness.
If we believe life is fundamentally bad or flawed, we
will be reluctant to quiet ourselves, afraid of meeting
the darkness that resides in things — or in ourselves.

In Genesis, a fundamental goodness is presumed
throughout the creation story. At every juncture, God
acts, steps back, and rests. God invokes the light,
separates it from the darkness. And so the story
continues, emptiness giving birth to form, with the
creation of living creatures, the beautiful birds that
claim the air as their home, the many-colored fish and
great whales, the cattle and insects, all the animals wild
and free upon the earth. Then God creates man and
woman in the likeness of God. And God saw
everything that He had made, and behold, it was very
good.

Wayne Muller, the author of the book *Sabbath:
Finding Rest, Renewal, and Delight in Our Busy Lives*,
said, "Since I was a child I have felt this fundamental
goodness in the world — in people, in life, in the earth. I
have felt the truth of this goodness even when no
external evidence suggested its presence. I gravitated

toward those forms of healing that presumed this essential strength and wisdom in people. I steadfastly believed, even as I worked in the midst of the most horrific sorrow, that there remained a persistent luminosity of spirit, an unquenchable resilience.

"Sabbath time assumes that if we step back and rest, we will see the wholeness in it all. We will naturally apprehend the good in how things are, taste the underlying strength, beauty and wisdom that lives even in the difficult days, take delight in the gift and blessing of being alive."

On the Sabbath we rest, and see that it is good.

Of the Spirit
Third Summer Vesper Service
Sunday, August 14, 2011: Deerfield Library
A Blessing For Elders

Elders are in the fifth quarter of the orange of life. In Joanne Harris's book, *Five Quarters of the Orange*, four children cut an orange into quarters and each ate an equal part. What was the fifth quarter? It was the peel, that part of the orange that is most colorful and fragrant, but the most disposable. It is generally not eaten by itself, but used to give extra flavor or aroma to other food or drink. It is the essence of the orange, the part that lingers on our hands, our tongues, and our senses. It should be the most important part, but instead is the least valued, the part most likely to be discarded.

Our lives have been neatly divided into four parts: childhood and youth, young adult, middle age, and the retirement years. Little attention has been given to the later years, particularly the eighties, nineties, and beyond. More and more people are experiencing this forgotten or ignored period of life. How sad to discount these valuable years!

The later years hold the greatest promise. Even with the decline of physical vigor and mental acuity that many people experience, the later years can be remarkably satisfying. Seeds planted early in our lives come to fruition. Life is a mystery novel with many answers withheld until the final chapter. There is no turning quickly to the last page to see how the story turns out. Our patience is tested many times, but finally the complex threads of the plot are revealed. Even if we don't like the outcome, knowing the answers is a comfort. Finally, we see the past in full flower, a rainbow of lights and darks that make up our life. The ultimate mystery is no longer frightening, but a natural final step of acceptance and peace.

We savor the smell, color, and texture of the orange peel. Perhaps it has none of the orange's original juice and firm flesh, but it is the perfect reflection of the original fruit's body, the tree that bore it, and the blossoms that signaled its beginning. It is diminished by time and use, but it is still valuable, to be saved and cherished. It holds the memories of the past and the dreams of the future. Elders are blessed to be the fifth quarter of the orange.

◆ ◆ ◆

Patience

Patience is my gift to hold and to share.

Patience is defined as "quiet, steady perseverance." I move confidently through each day with quiet, steady perseverance because my faith is strong. I know there is a time and a season for all things.

Patience is a gift to share. I cultivate it within myself and demonstrate patience at every opportunity.

Rejoice in hope, be patient. — Romans 12:12

From *The Daily Word*, July 7, 2011

Prayers Used in Women in Spiritual Exploration

All Knowing and All Powerful One,

Help us to celebrate and validate our essential common femaleness. Help us to learn the many languages of spirituality — our shared words, our powerful silence and our comforting and cleansing tears.

We are individuals who are one in the holy circle of life, engaged in our search to become one in God.

We pray for patience in our spiritual exploration. If we move only an inch in our search for enlightenment, at least we have moved. This is not a race. This is not a contest. This is an individual journey that cannot be measured by external signs or by comparison with others. It is ours to treasure and to move along at our own pace.

Thank you for giving us this day in our lives, for a place to share ourselves, to experience the power of silence, the warmth of human touch and voice, and the ultimate hope, to know God's love.

Amen.

Interfaith Prayer, Festival of the Family

Mother/Father God, Holy One,

Help us to understand those families whose identities are different from ours;

Help us to learn the multiple ways of loving, parenting, partnering, and working together for peace.

Help us to dare, to stand strongly against hate and issues that divide us, to encounter our differences with love and respect.

This we believe:

That love is stronger than hate,

That love is stronger than despair,

And that good is stronger than evil.

In the name of the One Who is loving and living, Amen.

Winter of Our Content 2011

At the risk of being thought an old fogie — well, you may think it, just don't tell me — I must admit that I am relieved when the holidays are over. I like much about the holidays, especially Christmas, but celebrating ending one year and starting another seems much ado about nothing. December 31 slides into January 1 without any assistance from me. The days and the years need to be numbered, I suppose, but I'll leave that task to others. Celebrating because one year is ending and another is beginning seems a trumped-up reason to throw a party and act foolish. Having to attend such parties is sufficient punishment, but having to appear to enjoy them is more than I can handle. Now if something really impressive could be done, such as reversing time, that would be noteworthy, and I would be there with a paper hat and noisy horn.

We greet each new year with hope and good wishes for health and happiness. Of course, we mean the good wishes, for the moment at least. Hope does spring eternal, and we know that the coming year will be better than the past. Everyone will be happier, healthier, kinder, gainfully employed, all bills paid, twenty pounds lighter, beloved by all. Strange to admit, but I believe all this will happen — next year.

◆ ◆ ◆

Have I told you recently how special you are to me? I look at the ads for other retirement facilities and they seem inviting and attractive. Why this one, then? It's because of you, my fellow residents. How fortunate I am to be spending my later years with the interesting, thoughtful, stimulating men and women who have chosen to come here. Our interconnectedness sustains us all.

Think of all the things we do together. We eat together, in relative harmony; we worship together, each in our own way. We learn each others' names and backgrounds, meet each others' families. We complain together, but not too frequently. We are sure that the "people downtown" do not understand or care about us. Also, we sew, decorate, mind the store, discuss books, take trips, read the weekly and monthly lists of activities and the myriad memos, share aches and pains, fears — real and imaginary — as well as feelings of loss, joy, depression, and hope.

All of these precious things enable us to live each day fully. Although we seldom speak of it, this new supportive extended family spares our own children and grandchildren from worry and guilt about our well being. Realize how blessed we are. Pat yourself on the back for being an integral part of this experiment of living to the end of our time. Perhaps no other generation or society has been so fortunate.

Thanks to all of you. God bless.

LOSS

Lament in a Time of Grief

Lord of the brokenhearted, You wept openly at the grave of your friend Lazarus, showing us once and for all that in every pain that rends the heart You have a part.

We grieve the loss of our parents, spouses, and friends who have gone on that final journey that we all shall face one day.

We know time does not heal our wounds, but makes them deeper. Bind up our wounds as we remember the wounds of Christ.

Make sacred the memories of those whom we have loved long since and lost.

Teach us to live in this world with kindness, where we only see dimly as in a mirror, until we join our loved ones who now see face to face.

Then we shall understand, even as we are fully understood, through the Wounded Healer, Jesus Christ.

Amen.

Facing Loss and Death

God of all comfort and hope, cradle all people everywhere who are feeling shattered by the loss of a loved one. Have mercy on all who feel deserted, abandoned, alone because mother or father, sister, brother, or life partner, child, or friend has died.

◆ ◆ ◆

This is a time to name your loss. As the basket of river rocks is passed to you, take one rock for each loved one you are remembering today. Hold it and say the person's name, silently or aloud. Either to yourself or aloud, say something about the person you have named. If you wish, say a silent prayer or a spoken one as you remember the person you have lost.

Pass the basket to the person beside you in the circle. When everyone has taken a rock, or more than one, let us remain silent for a few minutes. Together we will feel our grief, know it, and claim it.

◆ ◆ ◆

Thank you, God, for the bonds of kinship, the ties of friendship, the links of shared humanity that connect us to each other.

◆ ◆ ◆

We are not forced to take wings to find Him, but have only to seek solitude and to look within ourselves.

—Teresa of Avila

◆ ◆ ◆

They who wait for the Lord shall renew their strength, they shall mount up with wings like eagles, they shall run and not be weary, they shall walk and not faint.

—Isaiah 40:31

♦

He who lacks time to mourn, lacks time to mend.

—William Shakespeare

♦

As long as the earth endures, seedtime and harvest, cold and heat, summer and winter, day and night, shall not cease.

—Genesis 8:22

♦

Lo, the winter is past, the rain is over and gone,

The flowers appear on the earth, the time of singing has come,

And the voice of the turtledove is heard in our land.

—Song of Solomon 2:11-12

♦

Psalm 118 in the Bible contains this line: "I shall not die, but I shall live."

That's the message the spring of your grief contains: the discovery that, yes, you will live.

But it's more than a discovery–it's also a decision: "I shall not allow myself to die, but I shall choose to live again."

◆

Grief Melts Away

Grief melts away like snow in May, as if there were no such cold thing.

◆

Prayer of Thankfulness

Thank you, God, for making Yourself known to us in the seasons of the earth and the seasons of our lives.

Amen.

Prayer of Gratitude

Dear God, thank you for opening our hearts to acknowledge and name our losses. We are human, and we remember and grieve for those who have been a part of our lives and are gone. We are blessed to have known them. They are still a part of us and always will be.

We are grateful for our courage in times of sadness, remembering that we need not despair because help is always available to us if we ask. We are aware that grief is universal and we are a part of creation, and we all suffer loss and deep sadness.

We remember and give thanks for our interconnectedness with all we know and all we do not know. We feel love coming from the women in this circle today. The greatest expression of love is around us and among us as we seek for meaning in our world and our lives.

The greatest blessing is that we are not alone. There is a power which is always with us and to which we turn today and always. We are a part of the whole and the whole is good because it is God's creation.

May we trust that this season, like all others, will bear witness to God's extravagant love and faithfulness.

Amen.

Perplexing Thoughts

I wish someone would write a book of rules for widows and widowers. The question is, "How can we be friendly and not be seen as too interested, too aggressive, or too pushy?" My brother was warned after his wife died that he should bar his door to keep out the stream of widows who would come knocking. They would come bearing casseroles, exuding sympathy, eager to encourage him to replace her immediately.

Never a shy but often a tactless man, he managed to convince the well-meaning women that he didn't need or want a replacement for his late wife, that he didn't mind a sandwich alone at home or going out for a full meal. Also, he confided to me, there are cheaper and less intrusive ways to find another golf partner.

He was a very successful attorney in a city overpopulated with attorneys and had the house and possessions to display his success. To my dismay, he was also quick to anger, often abrasive, and politically incorrect. The hopeful women who knocked on his door were sure they could tame the tiger. I knew they couldn't. I loved him. I was his baby sister. The lines of women gradually decreased and he was alone. Contented? He seemed to be. A cautionary tale? Draw from it what you will.

◆ ◆ ◆

The Value of One

When I think of the number of people who have lived on Earth over thousands of years, is any individual important or worth our concern? I think so, but some days I wonder.

◆ ◆ ◆

Philosophy

Our book discussion group has just read an excellent book written by a professor of philosophy. I remember a classic question from Philosophy 101: "If a tree falls in a forest and there is no one around to hear it, will it make a noise when it hits the ground?"

A new question I just made up is this, "If I don't look, will the car speeding toward me still be there?"

The basic question, of course, is, "How do we know?"

Possessions

Today I am going to catalog the items in my curio cabinet. Some of the items have considerable monetary value and some only sentimental. Some I collected because I thought my children would like them and some because I enjoyed possessing them.

Recently there was a tag sale in an apartment near mine. I visited it out of curiosity rather than a need or desire for more stuff. My apartment runneth over. The former occupant and owner of the items for sale has downsized again, not in the final sense, but because his present apartment in the Health Center is quite small. He uses a hospital bed. The bed for sale was a king-sized one. He will not need it. Evidently, his family members do not either.

There were only a few other people at the sale while I was there. The three women managing the sale were courteous and businesslike, waiting for the afternoon closing hour. I looked in the living room, the bedrooms, kitchen, and closets. The items for sale were of good quality and very reasonably priced. I felt uncomfortable looking at them, as though I were invading the owner's privacy. After purchasing a few small items, I shut the door on his life and returned to my apartment with its things that my children don't want and I will not need.

Wouldn't a funeral pyre of things be kinder?

A WORKING LIFE

Helping Others

What I want to talk with you about is my role in helping others. I have spent a lot of my personal and professional life trying to help other people, usually women, through advising and counseling. I have recently begun to question why I have been so involved in other people's lives in this way and whether there is a dimension to my involvement that I have been unaware of.

My question is, "Is there a spiritual dimension in my attempts to help other people that I haven't realized or been aware of? Am I serving in a religious sense? To what extent am I my brother's (or sister's) keeper? What is our role as Christians in helping other people? What are the boundaries? What are my personal limits? What are my personal reasons for trying to help other people?

Abraham Lincoln said, "Time and advice are my stock in trade."

Advice giving is a huge industry in the United States. There are hundreds of books telling us what to do and not do. We are bombarded with advice on television, seminars, various groups, politicians, advertising, spiritual leaders, co-workers, columnists, human resource professionals, lawyers, parents, teachers, social workers, Dr. Phil on Oprah, and Larry King Live. What makes me think I can or should add to this chorus?

Advising and counseling have been and continue to be important practices in my life. I'm still at it! I'm working with a friend offering career counseling. My education and training in counseling has stretched over much of my life. Freud was still in fashion when I had my first psychology courses. Then I was indoctrinated into nondirective counseling with Dr. Carl Rogers. If a client asked the way to the library, I learned to respond, "I hear that you would like to go to the library." I learned to make the client take responsibility for the direction of the session. I remained nonjudgmental, totally accepting, remaining in the here and now, willing to go in whatever direction the client wished, unwilling to impose my beliefs or standards on the client. There were no absolutes, and I wondered if I had any beliefs of my own.

I was also exposed to behaviorism, which did not accept the mind, body, spirit concept. The point was to change the person's behavior so that he/she behaved in what was considered a more appropriate manner, at least according to the counselor. The counselor used rewards and punishments to bring about the desired changes. This is the approach often used with children, and it can be very effective. I was not comfortable with this system, but comfort was not a behavioral term.

I was introduced to directive counseling, but was not encouraged to utilize that approach. There the counselor tells the person what to do and how to do it. The counselor is in charge, and the assumption is that the counselor knows what is "best" for the client. This can be a very effective approach and is a "quick fix." It is a very popular approach, but may do little to encourage personal growth or the ability of the client to deal with other problems as they arise.

All of these approaches can be helpful and reflect the best intentions of the counselor, but they do not speak to my questions.

While I have been thinking about my personal reasons for wanting to help others, what triggered my thinking recently was the series of articles in our local newspaper about a man named Bob. He was a homeless man who was the object of much personal assistance by a farm family near Grinnell and a faculty member at Drake University and her husband. What interested me particularly were the various motivations of the individuals who attempted to "rescue" him from his homeless state and provide the stability and support that he said he wanted.

The farm family in Grinnell took in a homeless man. The man, Bob F., meets another couple and enchants them with stories of his colorful past: He was born to a prison inmate, never knew his parents, grew up in a state institution, and spent most of his adult life in prison. He became obsessed with Pam, an administrator at Drake University. Bob's behavior changes. He becomes incensed by a casual remark she makes. Pam and her husband, a former minister, offer to let Bob move in with them. Later, they and the Grinnell couple learn Bob has been telling lies to them.

His behavior becomes more erratic and threatening. He was never, of course, what he seemed to be.

But Bob is a mirage.

People see what they want to see.

To one couple, Bob is proof of faith's healing power.

To Pam, Bob is an example of why teachers should never lose faith in a student.

What was the religious basis for these people to try to help this man? The article said that the Grinnell couple relied on faith and common sense, but became unsteady and insecure as Bob's behavior worsened. The wife said that Bob's presence brought the family closer together. "I still hold that gift came to us in the form of Bob. I will hold to that forever, no matter what."

My question is, "Was she totally deluded, or did she have a very clear sense of her Christian faith?"

What is the basis for our responsibility to other people? What is the model that Jesus gives us for living our lives in ways that make people whole?

I remember the story of Cain and Abel from the Book of Genesis.

And Cain talked with Abel his brother and it came to pass, when they were in the field, that Cain rose up against Abel, his brother, and slew him.

And the Lord said unto Cain, "Where is Abel thy brother?" And he said, "I know not. Am I my brother's keeper?"

That question has resonated over the centuries.

I am currently asking, "What does it mean to use one's life to help others?"

I am asking this question as I respond to a woman's need for help and advice, even though I think she will not listen. I am convinced she is on a dangerous path that will lead to family disaster. Is it my business? How much risk should I take to try to help her?

I am left with more questions than answers. How can I discern the purpose of my life? What messages am I being sent? What messages am I missing?

Volunteer Vistas for Adult Women
Presented at Galaxy Conference on Adult Education
Washington, D.C., 1969

A few years ago, I accepted a position as Adult Program Associate at the Des Moines YWCA. When I did, I gave up my cherished status of volunteer for the different kind of status of professional staff member. My children asked me what I did on my new job. "Oh, talk on the telephone and go to meetings," I replied.

"And you get paid for that?" they exclaimed. "That's what you did anyway."

And they were right. My new job was basically the same kind of activity that I had been doing as a volunteer in various women's organizations, principally the American Association of University Women. I had done all the usual—and a few unusual—community activities that can fall the lot of the nonworking mother. In short, I was on everybody's list of available volunteers.

My progression from committee member to chairman to branch president to Iowa Division board member of AAUW caused little comment at home. My husband knows that I am easier to live with if I am busy and involved. The house may be dustier, but a cheerful wife is more important than a spotless house.

He did notice the numerous telephone calls and the increased expenses. Volunteers don't have office hours, as you know, and many calls come at meal times. The results of the untimely call may range from inconvenience to bedlam, but the caller seems blissfully unaware of the annoyed husband and hungry children.

My husband was also aware of the increasing pressure on me to attend functions no matter what the situation at home might be. The moderately involved volunteer can decide at the last minute not to attend. "Sorry, but I just can't make it tonight," are familiar words to any chairman. But when the gavel is in your hand, you go!

My volunteer assignment at the YWCA had been chairman of the annual Job Opportunities Clinic, a one-day workshop for women who wanted — or thought they wanted — to go to work. In accepting the staff position at the YW, I moved from the volunteer's chair to the other side of the desk, working on the clinic as part of my staff duties. I'm sure that my work as a volunteer was responsible for my being asked to take this job.

Working on the clinic was a learning experience for me. I began to understand the special needs of the "returning" woman — the in-out-in worker, as the employment service describes her. The woman who had never worked, or had not worked for a number of years, needed assistance before she was ready to look for a job. This assistance was not available to her, at least in our community.

It was this need that the sponsors of the Job Opportunities Clinic decided justified the expansion of the one-day event into an ongoing service, available whenever the woman was ready to use it. For the clinic to expand, more funds were needed. The YWCA would furnish staff time, office space, and telephone as well as clerical help. Each sponsoring organization voted to continue its annual contribution and to provide the necessary volunteers to develop and run the service.

The sponsoring organizations in addition to the YWCA were: Altrusa, the American Association of University Women, Business and Professional Women, Insurance Women of Des Moines, The Hawkeye Chapter of National Secretaries, Professional Women's League, Quota Club, Soroptimist Club, Wa TanYe, the Women's Department of the Greater Des Moines Chamber of Commerce, Women's Rotary, and Zonta.

Major funding came from a local foundation, the Sidney Mandelbaum Foundation. This funding for a two-year pilot program made it possible to offer the service without charge to any woman who sought it.

The need that we observed first-hand in the one-day clinics was best described in the March 1966 issue of *Women's Education*, as follows:

> The person most affected by the social changes of the last quarter century is the married woman whose family no longer demands most of her time and who feels a push and pull toward employment. She is not so much discontented as restless and she feels a need to earn money. She knows that she has knowledge, skills, energy,

and experience which, if put to use, could make her life more interesting and help her become a more useful citizen.

What she does not know is where to turn for help. She knows little or nothing about job opportunities, salary and wage scales, hours and working conditions, as well as skills and knowledge required. She does not know which of her talents or skills have any marketable value, what part of her life experience would count as an asset for an employer. She wonders whether she could learn new skills at her age, whether she could do herself justice in a testing or interview situation, whether she could hold her own with younger workers or men. She worries about how she would manage her household responsibilities, how her husband and children might feel about her job.

This description of the need proved to be accurate, except that the women who used our service were more unsure of themselves than the preceding paragraphs would suggest. A basic lack of confidence was present in almost every client, regardless of her educational level or age. Incidentally, the age range and the educational range were wider than we had expected them to be. The age range the first year was from twenty-two to seventy-six years. Most of the women were in the expected age range, however, from late thirties to early fifties. Their family responsibilities were lessening, and they were restless and thought they wanted to earn money. They wanted their lives to be more interesting, more useful, and more fulfilled. They also wanted a paycheck. A number of them said, "I have had it with volunteer work!"

The educational range of the women was from tenth grade through college graduate. The educational level seemed to have little bearing on their self-confidence, or their ability to establish a goal and work toward it. They were very unsure of their skills and abilities. The services that we provided them were: encouragement and moral support, accurate job and training information, referral to other community resources, and assistance in finding personal direction.

All of these aspects of the service, along with the mechanics of planning and developing it, were handled by volunteers. As the coordinator, I did the first interview with the client, which in some cases completed the woman's contact with the service. We explored the woman's problems and jointly decided upon her next step. If counseling seemed advisable, I made an appointment for her with a member of the counseling committee. Referral to other services, such as public or private employment services, might be offered. Answers to specific questions of "how to" were given, is possible. The various kinds of educational opportunities in the community would be discussed if this seemed appropriate. The woman's own needs and interest determined the extent and kind of service provided to her.

A committee of counselors was available by appointment to the clients of the service. All of the counselors were professionally trained women working in the fields of psychology, social work, or personnel work. There were twelve women who agreed to serve: eight social workers, three psychologists at the Master's level, and one personnel interviewer. A special consultant to the counseling committee was Dr. Marilee Fredericks, Director of the Des Moines Child Guidance Center.

In all, there were sixty-three volunteers connected with the service. Some gave a great deal of time, and others were only slightly involved. We tried to use their abilities well. We could not have purchased the time, the thought, and the effort these women gave as volunteers. I am convinced that they made a real contribution to the quality of life in our community. I know that they made a real difference in some women's lives.

In the summer of 1969, I was asked to join Drake University as Director of Women's Programs. I was to set up a program of continuing education for women. It was a difficult decision to make because I thoroughly enjoyed the YWCA program and was proud of its development. I did accept the offer, however, because I believe a woman can often fulfill her potential by means of a program of continuing education adapted to her personal needs and interests. I felt privileged to be appointed Assistant to the Dean of Continuing

Education at Drake University to design and implement this program.

Volunteers can provide an added dimension to any program. The Dean and I invited sixteen carefully selected men and women to serve as an advisory council for continuing education for women. The occupations represented in this planning group were: insurance professor, managing director of a credit union, a commissioner of the Iowa Employment Security Commission, president of a personnel agency, creative director of a publishing company, minister, coordinator of educational television, personnel assistant in a large insurance company, psychologist, college English instructor, housewife-graduate student, a professor emerita, training director at a large department store, and a young mother who was a former assistant dean of women. Impressive group!

We could not have afforded to hire these men and women, but they said they enjoyed being involved in developing this new program. I believe that in every community there are skilled and experienced people available for the asking, ready and willing to use their talent for a worthwhile program.

The kind of volunteering I am describing is a far cry from that usually offered the "willing worker." Volunteering is stereotyped as envelope stuffing, flower cart pushing, or collecting door-to-door for buck night. These jobs have to be done, and a beginning volunteer may need to do them before being offered something more interesting. Opportunities are present at many levels, however. If the person stays at the envelope stuffing level, either this is personally satisfying or she/he has failed to exhibit any sign of creativity or initiative.

In working with volunteers, I have tried to observe a few basic rules. Some I would recommend are:

1. Do not waste their time. Pre-plan what you hope to accomplish when they are with you.

2. Use volunteers in positions of authority and responsibility, as their abilities warrant.

3. If at all possible, find some expense money to cover actual out-of-pocket expenses. You will greatly expand your pool of available volunteers.

4. Use the volunteers in areas of their interests. Some will wish to volunteer in their professional area; others will want to do something different from their regular activities. Find out how they want to use their abilities.

5. If a volunteer does not function satisfactorily, change her job. Do not let an unproductive volunteer jeopardize a program.

6. Constantly train and promote volunteers. Doing "willing work" should be a continual learning experience.

7. Remember that words of praise and encouragement are essential. If you value the person's contribution, tell her/him so.

8. Don't apologize for asking a person to give time and talents to a worthwhile endeavor. One of the great problems of our time is the feeling of personal isolation and worthlessness. You may be enabling the person who volunteers to grow as an individual, to deepen his/her feeling of self-worth, and also to contribute something significant to the community.

Good luck with your volunteer program!

Old Speeches

Recently I have been reading old speeches I gave from 1967 into the 1980s, advocating a change in the treatment of women to bring them into full legal, economic, and social equality in this society. I used the arguments that I thought would be effective in bringing about this change.

The arguments were ones being made by many women leaders at that time of the beginning of the second women's movement. There was the dense prose of the so-called "mother of the modern women's movement," Betty Friedan, who pointed out the discomfort and "dis-ease" of many women. There was the voice of the deadly serious but brilliantly funny Gloria Steinem, whose sharp wit punctured myths, stereotypes, and complacency.

The Women's Bureau of the U.S. Department of Labor published statistics that proved the differences in women's treatment in an objective and seemingly undeniable way. The message was, "Here are the statistics. It is up to you to do something about these inequities."

Women's organizations gave a national voice to the effort in favor of women's rights. The one I am most familiar with is the American Association of University Women (AAUW). Its publications gave a legitimacy to the movement that had been lacking or overlooked by many women.

In the late '60s and early '70s, governor's commissions, as well as state and city commissions on the status of women were formed. Their members were usually appointed by the governor or mayor, giving them an official platform to hold public hearings, do research, get publicity, and establish ways for individual women and women's groups to make their messages heard without fear of reprisal. A national organization of commissions on the status of women was formed, which made it possible for issues to receive a national hearing, increasing the impact through numbers and breadth of the documented information.

Other women worked more privately; in consciousness-raising groups, church discussion groups, continuing education classes sponsored by educational institutions. There were also some radical groups who maintained that the root cause of women's subjugation was our paternalistic political system. They claimed that the system must be overturned by any means necessary before real equality of the sexes could ever be achieved. A small number of the women experimented with cooperative or communal living arrangements. These radical women were very bright, committed, usually young, and politically naïve.

The fringe groups that advocated abolishing our democratic form of government intrigued and stimulated me. They had the passion and vehemence that most of our meetings lacked. The most outrageous suggestion I heard was "take that chauvinist pig out and cut off his ..." I won't repeat what word was used, but the meaning was clear.

Sometime later, a friend of mine who had been deeply hurt by her lover told me that she had dreamed of doing just that to him. Fortunately, she found more socially acceptable ways to channel her anger. Her rage was directed at a particular male, while the rage of the radical women was directed at a male-dominated society. The similarity of the depth of feeling was startling and frightening, as was the suggestion of physical violence.

At that time, I believed that involvement in the women's movement was risky, and I still do. How much risk was I able and willing to take? I didn't know. Could I risk damage to my family, my marriage, my job, my friends and colleagues? Most hurtful would be the damage to my reputation. You have heard the comments made about feminists. Those remarks were deliberately hurtful, and often no one came to the woman's defense.

I doubt that it was bravery that kept me going. It was more likely stubbornness and a deeply felt sense of fairness. I knew that what was wrong in society for more than half of its members was not fair and must be changed.

In the early '70s, I had a brief blissful period when I thought everything was coming together and change would come soon. Perhaps the suffragists had a few times like that. But they persevered. They gave speeches and suffered imprisonment and ridicule. Ultimately, they prevailed, not easily and not quickly. We women honor them whenever we cast a ballot or tell our daughters, "Yes, you can." Their struggle was more easily defined than ours, but certainly not less important and difficult. We, too, will keep on speaking out and taking risks and applauding the advances women have made until equality is a reality for all women.

To all supporters of the women's struggle for equality and justice, both men and women, I say thank you and Godspeed.

Remarks on Receiving the
Distinguished Service Award
May 15, 1998

I came to Drake University in 1940, a shy seventeen-year-old freshman. My love affair with Drake was just beginning. It would last a lifetime.

Attending Drake was a dream, attainable because of a small scholarship and because I could live with my sister, her husband, and their baby near 42nd and University Avenue. As many others have done, I rode the streetcar on University to attend classes at my school. That "baby" is here with me tonight, considerably taller and grayer, along with my three children—all proud Drake graduates.

I "stopped out" twice before graduation, once to earn money and a second time to serve in the WAVES. I finally graduated in 1948. What a weekend this is for the Class of 1948!

Tonight I have been described as a pioneer in the struggle for equality for women. In the mid-1960s, this idea was met with considerable resistance, by women as well as men. Now, much has changed—and little has changed. It is important to look at what has been accomplished, and not be discouraged by what is yet to be done.

An advocate for social change rarely knows success, but often experiences discouragement and failure. Some people make this effort alone. In my case, I have been surrounded by family, friends, colleagues, and a great university to lend me strength and support. I have asked for help, and it has been given. I have asked for opportunities to serve, and they have been available to me. I have asked for total agreement with my views—and I have been reminded that humility is a virtue.

Tonight I do not need to be reminded to be humble. I have not made this journey alone. Drake has remained a central part of my life. Its campus still beckons, larger and more beautiful than ever. It still offers its riches—the search for knowledge, the friendships, the outstanding people who teach here and work here, the hope for a better future. Tonight, I am privileged to express my affection and respect for you and this university. Thank you to all of you, and to the others, living and dead, who have been part of my journey. I am very grateful.

—Betty Dillavou Durden

ILLNESS

A Chance Meeting

I had just left the church sanctuary following the Sunday service. The front hall was crowded with people, many greeting friends as they passed. It was warm and colorful, and I felt a part of a pleasant ritual as I moved along toward the Greenwood Room for coffee, cookies, and more fellowship.

Suddenly I saw a woman whom I knew — I had met her at a long-term care center. We had become acquainted when we were each visiting our husbands there. Her husband had Parkinson's disease, but at that time could still communicate reasonably well. My husband had Alzheimer's, but still retained some of his abilities. His word-finding skills had declined noticeably, and he was often confused and frustrated. She and I had talked as we arrived or left the health center and as we helped our husbands walk in the halls.

"Hello," I said, wishing I could remember her name. I had my church name badge on, but she did not. I didn't know whether she was a member.

"Good morning, it's good to see you," she replied with a pleasant smile.

"I haven't seen you for some time," I said. "You're looking well. How is your husband doing?"

"He died Thanksgiving Day," she replied quietly. "I'd like to tell you about his last days."

I was no longer aware of the other people in the hall. She knew that I had experienced the same loss.

"Tell me about it," I managed to say.

"We talked about everything," she said softly. "He didn't want any extreme measures, so I signed a paper instructing the nurses not to resuscitate him or do anything that would keep him alive if he had trouble breathing. He was ready to go."

"So you had the opportunity to talk about his wishes and followed them."

"Yes...I'm so grateful that he was lucid sometimes and that I could understand what he wanted. When our kids came, he couldn't talk to them. I'm not sure he knew them."

The people in the hall walked by us, and I just stood and listened because she needed to tell me how it was. I was surprised to feel tears starting. I seldom cry. She could tell that I was feeling her grief, but I was also feeling my own.

What did I say to her? What should I have said? It had been almost five years since my husband died. Her words brought back my pain as she was bravely telling about her recent loss. I realized I was still angry... angry at my husband for leaving me, at the doctors for saying there was nothing they could do, at my children for accepting his death when I could not and most of all, at God for letting this happen. Was this part of His plan? Is there any plan? Does He know or care about our lives?

We were just two older women talking softly in the church corridor, acknowledging each other's sorrow. What more could I say or do for her and for myself? What more could the church do? Two widows, alone, trying to comfort each other while looking into the abyss.

A Voice from the Heartland

This is an ordinary day, for which I am grateful. Today I woke at my usual time, opened my blinds to enjoy a sunny day, stepped out on my balcony, retrieved the newspaper outside my front door, and enjoyed my customary early morning activities. My breakfast tasted good, even though it looked a lot like chicken feed. I sniffed the milk before I poured it, a habit from feeding children so many years ago. An ordinary day.

Yesterday was not an ordinary day. It had required planning and a consultation (consult, as they call it) with a surgeon. "It's time we find out what's causing your problems," my family doctor had declared. At least he didn't say that I had aches and pains because I was old, though that was true, too.

So the diagnostic process began. It was a "rule-out" process, the medical people explained to me. They start at the top, meaning with the worst possibility, and go progressively lower until they find what appears to be the cause of the problem. That sounded like a reasonable approach to me.

In my case, the top (worst) possibility was _____. Determining whether I had whatever that was required a biopsy of an artery at my left temple. To the surgeon, this was a quick and easy procedure. To me, it was a frightening one. It involved a small incision to reach the artery, then removal of a small piece of the vessel to send to the laboratory for testing, then a simple closure of the opening.

It did not sound simple or painless to me. After all, it was my head this unknown man would be cutting into. Arteries carry lots of blood, I was sure. Would I bleed a lot? My active imagination painted a frightening picture of possible outcomes. I would be permanently scarred at the least and blinded at the worst. Whoever said ignorance was bliss?

The unknown surgeon turned out to be a gentle little man who explained in great detail what he would be doing during the procedure and how I would feel. "You'll be under local anesthetic," he said, "so you'll feel pressure but no pain. I'll seal the ends of the artery and there will be very little bleeding. You'll have a small purple line at your temple when we're through. You can wear a red hat with it. When you're old you can wear purple."

Great, I thought. *You'd better stick to surgery, not poetry.* His kind intention was to reassure a nervous old lady and it worked…pretty well.

During the procedure, the surgeon occasionally asked me how things were going. He seemed pleased when I replied, "Fine." Later my daughter asked if he knew that "fine" was the female "F" word. He probably didn't.

All went well, despite our communication disconnect. My "awake" condition allowed me to hear the chatter in the operating room. It was not up to

"M*A*S*H" levels. The doctor wanted to be with his wife, who was vacationing in Arizona. The assisting women wanted to be home getting ready for the July 4th holiday. I wanted to be anywhere else.

The surgeon is probably sitting on a mountain in Arizona, the women are recovering from the stress and fun of a family gathering, and I am back in my apartment with a purple stripe on my left temple. I do not plan to buy a red hat. Whatever the worst possibility was, I do not have it.

Acceptance

I can't remember your name.

Some days, I can hardly remember mine.

I look in the mirror and see a strange lady,

Not very attractive.

I look down and there she is.

My mind is fading into the mist.

Who am I? Only God knows for sure.

Soon the mist will swallow me and I will be gone.

I don't mind.

Don't weep. I am at peace.

Written for an Alzheimer's patient

Lines about Feeling Old

Sometimes I use feeling old as an excuse. I'm too old to read a long book, to straighten my closet, to write some thank you notes, to learn to use e-mail. No one will notice, I think. If I want to take a nap instead of do exercises, I'm entitled. Who will know or care?

The people walking in the halls of our retirement community smile and greet me, but don't motivate me. The exercisers in the wellness room concentrate on their efforts, and I turn my head away. The friends at dinner who decline the piece of cake or pie make me think that I should do the same. But I don't. I'm old. Who cares if my clothes are getting tighter or my steps slower? I don't have a full-length mirror, and I'm certainly not going to get one. I can't read the numbers on the scale anymore, thank goodness. Why should I care? I'm old.

Our daughters don't notice how we look, do they? If so, they don't say anything. Sometimes they offer to take us shopping for a new outfit, but that is such an effort. This pantsuit still feels okay. I'm not sure how long I've had it, but I still like it. It makes me feel like me. What is my daughter seeing that I'm not? Is my son thinking that I'm seeming a bit slower this year? Are my grandchildren wondering if I still care how I look? Maybe they're not coming to visit me as often because I look old and act old.

I intend to change. Starting now, I'm going to read something that I don't agree with and think about it.

I'm going to call a friend and have a good visit. I'm going to invite a new friend to eat with me. I may even go shopping.

For my own sake, I'm going to be a livelier and more interesting person. If my knees hurt, you won't know it. If I'm sad about something, I'll say, "So be it." I'll learn a new prayer and think about my beliefs in a new way. I may even join the hall walkers. Who will notice? I will. And I'll bet you will too.

The Unwelcome Guest

I live with Pain. Maybe you do too. When I wake up in the morning, I wonder if Pain will be with me today. He usually is. He seldom goes away all day, leaving me in peace. In the evening, he is always with me—in my shoulders, down my back, adding an unpleasant sensation to my stiff legs.

In the morning, before I'm ready to get out of bed, Pain comes in the form of leg cramps, making me hang onto the foot of the bed and gingerly putting weight on the aching leg, trying to straighten the cramping muscles. When I complain, Pain laughs and says it is a very effective way to get me up. I do not see the humor in this.

As I get washed and dressed for the day, I try to ignore Pain. He is leaning lightly on my shoulders and arms but when I lift them to comb my hair, he gives me a sudden jolt. "Don't think you're free of me," he says.

Preparing breakfast requires very little stooping or lifting, so Pain does not demand much attention. Cutting a melon brings him back as I try to bend my fingers with their lumpy joints. Pouring cereal into the bowl is easy and dropping the bread into the toaster sometimes escapes his attention. "I am free," I think, until I try to pull the chair out so I can lower myself into it. I eat slowly, grateful to be able to feed myself. It's just discomfort I'm feeling, I reassure myself, not real pain.

I wondered how other people were dealing with pain. When I told my dinner companions recently that I was trying to write some humorous comments about pain, they looked amazed. "Pain is not funny," they told me. "It's like an unwelcome guest who comes and stays and won't leave," one woman explained.

A man at the table commented, "I have my own system for taking care of pain. At bedtime, I massage my kneecaps, moving them around a bit. Then I do a special foot treatment. It helps. At least I think it helps. Of course, pain is still there, just not so bad. Maybe it's all in my head, but I don't think so."

"I can't think of anything funny about pain," the third person said. "It's just something we live with."

My dinner companions weren't much help and I told them so. I asked if they had any tricks they used when Pain sat with them in their most comfortable chair or climbed into bed with them and wouldn't let them sleep.

"No, I just grin and bear it," said one.

"I try to rate the pain like they do in the hospital, from one to ten. One is the least and ten is the most. Is it a four today, or is it a five? A gall bladder attack is an eight, kidney stones rate a nine, and childbirth deserves a ten. Today may only be a four. I can handle that. I've had worse," one woman explained. "Rating it puts it into perspective."

To me, Pain is an interloper, an invader, a damned nuisance. Worse than my boring Uncle Harry. My mother said we had to put up with him, but he set my teeth on edge. She also said we were not to cry when we fell and got hurt. The pain would go away and we were building character. Now the pain doesn't go away and I have all the character I can stand.

To me, Pain is a family member, an in-law I never liked. I should be used to him by now, but he can still irritate me. Sometimes when I turn suddenly, it feels as though he stabs me in the heart. Other times, he takes my breath away. Sometimes he's just there beside me, a constant presence. Other times, he drives me to drink, literally, but that just adds more pain. I don't want to become addicted to pain pills, but that might not be so bad.

I wonder how I could get rid of him, separate my pain-filled body from my mind. Perhaps meditation could help me do that. I can imagine floating serenely above my aching body, feeling nothing but lightness and warmth. That would show him. He could be his most obnoxious and I wouldn't even be aware that he was there. But where would I be?

Avoidance of pain is a human desire, I realize, but it may not be possible or even desirable. Old muscles ache, old bones break, old lungs gasp for breath, old hearts pound.

Old bodies feel pain and bear pain as a part of life. We have learned how to be strong and brave whether we want to or not. The stabbing pain eases, the bones heal, the tense muscles loosen, the pain medication soothes. We know that the unwelcome guest is still with us, but we also know what to expect. We know we can handle what he dishes out.

My dinner companions were right. There's nothing funny about pain.

> Nature is merciful and does not try her children, man or beast, beyond their compass. It is only when the cruelty of man intervenes that hellish torments appear. For the rest, live dangerously, take things as they come.

> Fear naught, all will be well.

Paul Johnson; *Churchill*. Published by the Penguin Group, 2009.

Dedicated to all those who carry their pain with grace and dignity…

With affection and admiration.

HUMOR

Ironing

I seldom iron. Along with other housewifely tasks, ironing was one of the first to go. I am no longer a wife, nor do I have a house. There has come a time, however, in my peaceful and task-free life, when ironing is required.

Recently, in a fit of enforced deep cleaning, I sorted through some tablecloths that had been carefully stored away. Their condition was acceptable until I examined a lovely old lace cloth. To my horror, in its folds I found reddish stains of unknown origin. I would never have put it away with food stains on it! What had caused this disaster and what could be done to salvage the cloth?

This lace cloth was a treasured family heirloom inherited from my sister. She had purchased it in Granada, Spain, on a trip we took together many years ago. Some of the lessons she taught me about traveling were not to whine about the food and always to have my luggage outside the door by the appointed time. By example, she taught me to buy one special item on each trip. Her special purchase in Spain was the large handmade lace tablecloth. When I found the stain on the cloth, I felt that I had defiled her memory.

Since I had no idea how to attack the unknown stains, I visited a lace shop in Valley Junction, taking the cloth along to show. The young woman shopkeeper examined the disaster. She had faced such a problem before and showed me a stain remover liquid that had worked for her. Her instructions were to soak the cloth in water with a small amount of this liquid. "Soak the cloth for two or three days before washing," she told me.

To my enormous relief and some surprise, the stains disappeared as she had predicted. A gentle washing completed the process. I was left with a very clean tablecloth that needed ironing. Although I was tempted to send it to the cleaners down the street, I decided to do it myself. This unwise decision was probably to atone for my sin of neglect of this valued possession.

After moving into my retirement home, I bought an inexpensive (cheap) ironing board and a new iron. On a recent Labor Day, I decided to tackle the last step of the restoration of the tablecloth. Labor Day seemed an appropriate day since I had always thought the proper way to honor the laborers of the world was to join them. The prevailing notion of showing respect for their efforts is to take a day off from work.

Carefully I set up the ironing board in the kitchen, where the linoleum floor provided the most stable base for an unstable board. I plugged the iron in what I thought was a working outlet. It was not. Another attempt disconnected my clock, causing me to spend considerable time resetting it. Finally, I unplugged the toaster and plugged in my new iron.

Any new appliance comes with instructions for its correct and safe use. As a survivor of assembling children's toys, I always read the instructions. As I remember, they used to be relatively understandable. That was in the good old days. Now the instructions are a challenge. The instruction packet showed that this iron had thirteen identifiable parts, all neatly diagrammed and numbered. My old iron had a dial to turn it on to the desired temperature and an opening for the distilled water. The new one had a spray organ, a filler door, a spray button, a shot steam button, a cord bushing, and several other items that I chose to ignore.

My new iron was manufactured in China. Probably the instructions were written by an earnest young Chinese person who had taken English in school. The opportunity to actually speak English would be limited, of course. The result was a five-page list of instructions that I found confusing and demeaning. The person who had written the directions obviously felt strongly about safety. So did I, for that matter. Under the heading "Vertically Ironing," Point 4 cautioned, "Never use it in a garment put on a person, do it on a hanger. Bear in mind that the steam that takes place is to very high temperature and in this position you upset if it is visible."

Reinforcing these excellent cautions, the next note read, "To avoid accidents carry to extremes the precautions in this way of use." Another note read, "Before cleaning the iron in any way, make sure that the appliance plug is not connected to the socket."

All of these points seemed reasonable to me, if a little obvious. Perhaps current irons are more sensitive than the one I had used for many years. I skipped most of the cleaning instructions after trying to decipher this point, "Introduce the rod in the liquid and make it plunged for 4 hours approximately. Then extract the rod, rinsing the end with water of the faucet and it return to placing in the plate."

After carefully ironing the lace tablecloth, being mindful of all the warnings and instructions for safe usage, I read, "How to Put it Away." The first line told me to "Disconnect the plug of the iron from the socket." Since I had never put an iron away while it was still connected to the plug, I agreed with that point. I did wonder, however, the assumed mental capacity of the user of this iron. Somewhere, an anxious manufacturer must have said, "We have to tell these Americans everything. They don't trust us to manufacture a good product. They think everything they make is better just because it costs more. Maybe we should charge more for ours."

Perhaps you now understand why I have decided to give up ironing entirely.

Sleepwear or Lack Thereof

I am sleeping in torn pajamas. It's not that I particularly like torn pajamas or much care what I sleep in, but I have discovered the current price of comparable new ones. Recently, I went to a favorite store of mine to purchase new pajamas. I found some quite acceptable ones, then looked at the price tag. Unable to believe my eyes, I asked for assistance. The tag read $150! What went with them, I wondered. Perhaps a robe? But no, the pleasant clerk assured me. The tag was correct. The pajamas cost $150.

What would cause my family more alarm, for me to pay that price or continue to sleep in my comfortable but worn-out pajamas? Either way, they would consider me eccentric or worse. My daughter would say she could find some at a much cheaper price. My business-savvy son would give me a lecture on current and future market conditions and advise me to buy the new pair before the price went up or the market collapsed. I would not consult my older son. He might think I should sue the store and the manufacturer for shoddy merchandise and misleading advertising. I don't want to do that.

I am in a quandary. In the meantime, I have found a soft old nightgown I had forgotten. It will do quite well until we are all issued identical pajamas made in China. Who will care if all the buttons are hanging on by one thread? After all, who is going to see my pajamas? There is always some comfort in living alone.

If I am taken to the hospital in the night, please look the other way. Of course, the way the economy is going, we all may be wearing torn pajamas. At least I'll be used to them.

Things I Learned While Traveling in the Low Countries

Don't try to speak Dutch while facing your companion. He will not appreciate a warm spittle bath.

Don't try to speak Dutch. Don't count on the basic good nature of the Dutch to help you speak that language. They will switch to English and suggest that you do the same.

Also, don't complain about the high taxes in America. The European response will be instructive but not pretty.

Don't tell a Dutchman that his house would look better if it were wider and didn't lean toward the street. Also, don't tell a Dutchman that the builder forgot to remove the hook between the small windows at the top of his house. He will want to know how you get your furniture to the third or fourth floor of your house. Working out this conundrum will be harder than establishing NATO.

Don't ask a Dutchman how his fields can be lower than the canal beside it. Your eyes will glaze over and he will still be explaining it to you with hand gestures, digging motions, and waving his arms like a windmill. You will still not understand it because it is basically impossible.

Don't ask a tour guide to tell you if the vase you chose is an authentic piece of Delft. You will be taken to a cramped corner of an old building where a nice young man will explain that his family has been in the business of producing Delft for five generations. His pieces are hand painted, hand glazed, handmade from the best materials and totally authentic, as this certificate from the local Chamber of Commerce will attest. Evidently, the natives of Morocco are to Delft porcelain as the Chinese are to U.S. products. They claim a vase is hand painted if they painted three lines on it and then transferred the design to the blank sides. Such indignity!

It does not take much effort for Dutch speakers to spit on everything within a three-foot radius, so be sure to sit in the back of the room. They do it with abandon when describing the nefarious practices of those North African scoundrels who copy their glorious Delft pieces. The speaker will still be describing the marks of authenticity on the bottom of the vase from his factory as you slip quietly away.

Other impressions:

The streets are narrow to encourage bicycling and discourage car traffic. Even if you manage to maneuver a car down the streets (we would call them alleys), you will have to go back home because there will not be a place to park and you couldn't afford one anyway. Besides, gas costs about $8 (in our money, but who knows how much in euros). This is per liter, but you don't know whether that is more or less than a gallon. Don't ask for a conversion chart for dollars and euros. You won't want to know.

Bicycles are growing in exponential numbers. They are practical and the Dutch love practicality. They are cheap to ride (not to buy) and parking is cheap, which is the only amount the Dutch really like. Your first bike may be quite expensive, but by the time your bike has been stolen three or four times, you will replace it with a much cheaper model or simply steal someone else's. Replacing your stolen one with one that is available on the street makes a good deal of sense. It has something to do with making life fairer. Even the Calvinist Dutch can come to terms with this logic.

Don't comment on the weather if it is raining. Of course it is raining. Now if the sun is shining, feel free to describe the beautiful blue sky, the sparkling water in the rivers, canals, dikes, North Sea, or the puddles left from yesterday's rain. It is hard for a Dutchman to express joy or even mild pleasure, but a sunny day will make even a Calvinist smile quietly behind his hand. This small expression of delight may bring into question the person's ultimate reward, but if that has already been predetermined, what's the problem?

Thoughts on Same-Sex Marriage in Iowa

Hooray! I no longer have to marry a man. The Iowa Supreme Court ruling approving same-sex marriages significantly increased my options for remarriage. It doesn't say that a person must be homosexual to marry a person of the same sex, just that you have the right to do so if you choose.

What a relief! Should I, a very senior widow, decide that I would like to remarry, the numbers are now in my favor. In my retirement community, women outnumber men about four to one. This is consistent with national figures.

Now that I am legally allowed to marry either a man or a woman, my chances of finding a mate have improved enormously. Every evening I dine with various attractive women. I had never considered them as marriage partners, but that may change. At our ages, marriage is primarily about companionship anyway.

The world as we know it is designed for couples. Dining tables seat two, four, or six people. Should a man sit with three or five women, other diners either congratulate him on his "harem" or commiserate on his bad luck. He pretends not to mind sitting with the "girls" but escapes as soon as possible after the meal.

My daughter, who practices family law, will notice some changes with single-sex marriage. With traditional marriage, there has always been the unexpected consequence of divorce. This will be as true for same-sex couples as for traditional ones. The issues may be the same, but the assumptions will change. In the case of child custody, which "mother" or which "father" will be seen as the one to be designated as custodial parent? What will be the criteria? The courts' assumption that the mother is awarded custody will have to be reviewed. What if there are two mothers or no mothers?

What about other issues? The question of alimony, child support, single or joint custody, visitation rights, college tuition, ownership of items purchased prior to the marriage or purchased jointly, will have to be worked out by looking through a slightly different lens. Inheritance rights may not be so clear. Who is the head of the household? What constitutes a family? These questions will require new thinking and some new laws, as well as a seismic shift in society's beliefs.

These issues don't worry me. They excite and challenge my thinking, my assumptions, my basic beliefs. They reassure me that I am alive and able to grow and change. Here are some random thoughts about these issues:

- Who is a real man, one who is married to a woman or to another man? Could it be either?

- If marriage is only for procreation, why is woman's ability to bear children so much shorter than her marriage may last?

♦ If your granddaughter marries a woman or
   your grandson marries a man, do you attend
   the ceremony? That is your decision, though
   your absence would be noted and
   commented upon. Send a gift and your love
   anyway.

♦ Women seldom snore as loudly as men. This
   is an assumption based on lack of personal
   research. I am not an expert on this subject,
   or any other, for that matter.

♦ Separate this legal decision from religious
   positions. If your religious beliefs support
   marriage for a man and a woman only, you
   still have a right to believe that. You can
   control and believe what you wish. Can you
   force your beliefs on all the citizens of this
   diverse country? Perhaps it is only arrogance
   that makes us try.

♦ Remember that God speaks to all of us,
   according to our own ability to hear and
   understand. My church says that God is still
   speaking. Change is a part of life. I hope we
   can listen with open ears and loving hearts.
   Maybe there is a new message just waiting
   for us to hear.

Who is Kate Spade?

For many years, I have been perfectly contented with my purses. I thought them quite smart. They used to have to match my shoes, but that is no longer required. My purchase range for a new purse was from about $40 up to, but not exceeding, $60.

All was well until my daughter took a good look at my outfit, purse included, and decided that I was significantly "underpursed." First, she sent my sixteen-year-old granddaughter shopping with me. We looked at every purse at Von Maur, Younkers, Dillards, and some little shops in the mall. There were hundreds of purses. Many appealed to my granddaughter, very few to me. They were too large, too colorful, too strangely shaped, but primarily too expensive.

Many years ago, my husband was sent on Navy Reserve duty in Florida. When he returned, he proudly presented me with a gift. It was a real crocodile-skin purse—complete with the creature's head on it! I had to carry it a couple of times before I could hide it in the back of my closet.

After the unsuccessful shopping excursion with my granddaughter, my daughter decided to find a suitable purse for me. She presented her gift in a large, expensively wrapped box. Inside was a cloth bag with a drawstring closure. Inside the bag was a gray leather purse. The leather was snake or possibly crocodile—real, of course. I examined the purse with trepidation. It had a woman's name on it.

"There's been a mistake," I said. "This purse belongs to Kate Spade. Here's her name printed on it. You must find her and return it to her."

My granddaughter rolled on the floor laughing. My daughter was horrified at my ignorance of fashion. I was clueless, but I knew I was in for another tutorial on style and famous designers.

Actually, I learned to like the purse. I carry it quite frequently and wear my comfortable gray SAS shoes with it. My shoes and purse match, sort of. I am still not acquainted with Kate Spade.

My search for style was in remission for a while. Then last summer, I joined other Deerfield women on a bus trip to the East Village, where we were allowed to roam from one little shop to another. Overwhelmed with this unexpected freedom, I stopped in a little coffee bar. My usual choices of coffee consist of regular or decaf. This was not sufficient for the East Village. At last, the young man behind the counter and I came to an agreement about a suitably trendy beverage. It cost about $4, but it came with a table and chair. I was much refreshed by all this, especially the attention of the young man. He seemed very interested in my reaction to his concoction. It was hot and tasty, but not really as good as Deerfield coffee. I did not tell him that.

The shop next door drew me in. I was pleased to see the owner of the Italian store from Valley Junction. He had moved to the East Village some time ago, and seemed depressed that I had not heard that momentous news. His new shop had the same attractive merchandise I remembered from his former location. There were lovely silk scarves, costume jewelry, gift items imported from Italy, and PURSES. One purse caught my eye. I circled the shop, hoping to ignore it. My circle brought me right back to that purse. It was gorgeous. Cautiously, I asked the young woman clerk its price. I knew I could not resist the charms of the purse and the handsome Italian owner. The price was about five times what I normally pay for a purse. I did my usual delaying tactic, a walk to the next store to clear my mind.

Was the purse as beautiful as I thought it was? I had to go back to look at it again. There it was in its full exotic glory, a generous-sized shoulder bag in a handsome combination of black and brown. There were highlights of green and beige and touches of flame and blue in a distinctive Middle Eastern design. The embroidery was hand done on silk, and the leather was buttery soft.

The other women on our tour had by this time gathered in the little Italian shop, watching me as I examined this work of art. Almost as one, they said I must have it. "It's your colors," one said. "It is great with the outfit you have on," another woman proclaimed. Overwhelmed by their approval, I turned to the clerk and said, "I'll take it."

These women are welcome to go shopping with me anytime. My wardrobe will improve, but my charge card balance will greatly increase. The purse is carefully stored in my closet. I look at it occasionally and appreciate its elegance. It is still in pristine condition. I have not yet actually carried it, perhaps waiting for an occasion worthy of its beauty. One of these days, the time will be right. My outfit will blend with its unusual color scheme, I will be having a good hair day, my coat will look new, and I will have found both of my matching gloves.

When that magic moment comes, I will remember that day when my Deerfield friends gave me their blessings to buy a lovely purse. They said I was worth it. By the way, I still don't know Kate Spade.

Father,

before I close my eyes

in this night's dark,

I pray for sleep that restores and refreshes,

for dream that restores in its releases;

and may I be serene in this dark passage

in knowing I am in Your care watched over,

in the calm of Your arms beyond harm, alarm,

entirely abandoned to You,

body and soul.

NATURE

Beautiful October

This early October day was one to cherish. To mark it in my memory, I drove west and then north through the countryside, savoring the beauty of the end of the growing season and completion of the harvest in this fertile central Iowa land.

Some of the fields were almost empty. Some still had corn stalks standing, but the ears had been removed by the harvesting machines. I remember when that hot and difficult job was done by hand. No longer. What do the men who drive the machines brag about now, how many bushels they can gather? There is still pride in the job, I'm sure. No matter how it is done, the result is the same. The Iowa gold is removed from the field and trucked away or stored until it is ready for market.

Today the wind was blowing the flags straight out from their poles, bending the young trees and sending a cloud of dust from the fields. Some of the leaves were showering down to lie in colorful heaps on the dry lawns and in the ditches. The trees glowed with their fall colors: yellow, red, burnt orange, gold.

I traveled smoothly over the two-lane roads, flat or gently rolling. There was almost no traffic and the roadwork was done for the week. The whole world was holding its breath, savoring the completed work and the sunny, warm day. *Enjoy it now,* it seemed to be saying. The land will lie fallow, the snows will bring the needed moisture, and another season will be upon us.

Each season has its own beauty, but October is a masterpiece.

◆

In August, I sold the vacation house that was my destination on my scenic trips through the Iowa countryside. It was only fifty-five miles from my retirement apartment, an easy and relaxing trip — except in winter. As I envisioned another hard winter like the last one, I wondered if I would be able to make many trips to my house. Talking with a real estate man, I learned that the housing market was very slow, just as it was in most parts of the country. "Expect it to take about a year for your house to sell," he warned me. Five days after listing it, he called me. "You have an offer," he said. Since the offer was at the listed price, there were no negotiations. I was both delighted and sad, having expected to use the house during the waiting period. A rush to clear out the house and garage overwhelmed me.

Now successfully through that challenge, I realize the decision to sell was a good one.

I had purchased the house a few months before moving into Deerfield. It allowed me to keep many of my things that my new apartment would not hold. The small central Iowa town where I graduated from high school so many years ago was still attractive, with a Norman Rockwell flavor. While I viewed it with affection, I looked for evidence of its ability to withstand the forces that were diminishing small towns everywhere. Sadly, I found few. What will reinvigorate Iowa's small cities and towns? I hope the university researchers are working on this problem.

◆

We search for beauty, perfection, and permanence. We want the beauty of this season to remain, although we know it is a time of transition. To live fully, we must treasure the moment. Life is about change. The beauty of a small Iowa town, of this colorful season, or our own imperfect handiwork all contribute to life's pattern. Even the mistakes are part of the beauty. Enjoy!

Bonds

More snow blew in last night to add another layer to our already white world. The lake, which was not completely frozen yesterday, is now hidden under a white blanket. The service road, which curves around the lake and disappears behind the west wing of our retirement facility, has been plowed, but nothing is moving on its slick surface.

Yesterday the Canada geese huddled together in a circle of open water on the lake. There were between forty and fifty of them sitting in the freezing water, not separated into couples as usual but part of a mass of black, white, and gray. Recently they had lifted off to seek a warmer climate, or so I thought. Yet some birds remained, probably shivering in the frigid water.

I dressed quickly, thinking of the cold, wet, and probably hungry geese. Why were they still here? Today there is no open water for them to rest in. Where do they land and huddle together when their world becomes ice and snow covered?

Yesterday our Birders group watched a movie called *March of the Penguins*, a documentary of the life of the Emperor penguins at the South Pole. These large birds live in the incredibly harsh climate at the bottom of the world. There they follow their ancient journey returning to the area of their birth. There they find a mate and lay one egg, nurturing it for months until the life inside cracks open the shell and emerges. Both parents take turns protecting this fragile life, producing another generation of these magnificent flightless birds.

As I walked through the silent halls on my floor this morning, I felt alone in a crystal, cold world. I needed people to remind me that I was a part of this retirement community. A small group was gathering in the sunroom by the elevator, and someone invited me to join the meeting, saying it was an Episcopal service and I was welcome. They knew I was not a member of that denomination, but they welcomed me anyway.

I descended from the fourth floor to the second, where there is always activity. The two people behind the reception desk greeted me in their usual friendly and courteous way. The desk clerk is a cheery anchor of sanity and calm, dealing with the many demands of her job. She knows us residents by name, even recognizing our voices on the telephone. We need her and, amazingly, she seems to need us.

Continuing down the hall, past the usually busy game room, I entered the beauty shop. The beautician greeted me but paused to direct a man to Assisted Living before starting my shampoo. The next client was another resident who was brought to the shop in her wheelchair. She was frail with skin nearly as white as her hair. Elegantly dressed in soft gray trousers and lilac sweater set, she was as beautiful in her advanced years as she must have been as a young woman. I had frequently walked behind her and her attentive husband as he pushed her wheelchair in the hall.

Conservatively dressed in wool trousers and beige cashmere jacket, he matched her elegance. They were a matched set, mated for life.

What is this glue that binds two creatures together? It is not just procreation, though that is a powerful force. The man and woman were long past the years of bearing and caring for children. The Canada geese that I watched from my apartment had probably cared for their chicks during several seasons and might do so again. There were no chicks to require their care during the cold winter months.

The Emperor penguin couple survived the deadly months of hunger, frigid weather, and isolation to bear and nourish their one chick. Next season, thousands of other pairs will continue the ancient ritual.

The bonds that connect us to each other, whether human or bird, are as strong as steel, fine as spider webs. They may be invisible or they may glisten in the light. Some miraculous force binds us together in the incomprehensible dance of life. We are part of the past and the future. Let us be grateful for this gift.

Japanese Beetles:
Lines from an Invasion
on the Fourth Floor

This morning, my apartment was invaded by a Japanese beetle. This tiny bug looks like a ladybug, but it's no lady. This small creature's ancestors made the long journey from Japan into eastern North America, possibly as welcome immigrants. As a grub, they feed on the roots of grasses and decaying vegetation and as adults, they eat foliage and fruits. What it found to eat on my window shade, I do not know.

I regarded the ladybug with concern. It disregarded me and continued to walk across the window blind as though it had a destination in mind. I decided to speak directly to it/him, making it clear that I wished him to leave immediately. I even informed him that I did not like him, even though he was a rather cute little bug. I had purchased this apartment at considerable expense, and I did not want another occupant unless he was paying half the monthly fee.

Giving no evidence that he would consider such an arrangement, he continued his journey across the blind. I determined to be ruthless. Just how to do this, I wasn't sure. I considered picking him up and tossing him out my balcony door. I suspected him of being capable of crawling back inside, needing only a tiny opening for his miniscule body. I rejected crushing him under my foot since I would then have to dispose of his lifeless, but hard-shelled, little body. What to do?

Finally, I decided on a less than courageous choice. Holding a piece of toilet paper in my hand, I picked up my unwelcome visitor and carried him into the bathroom. Probably he can swim, I thought, and dropped him into the toilet. When I checked later, he was indeed swimming in the water, apparently determined to survive. I exercised my determination to be permanently rid of him against his determination to prevail and flushed him down.

I was rather glad that he could swim, but I didn't want him swimming in my neighborhood. I have nothing against him personally, but you know how his kind are. They reproduce too rapidly. They have their own language and it isn't English. If they can fly up to a fourth-floor apartment, a fence probably would not keep them out. One is cute, but hundreds, thousands, who knows how many, are not acceptable. That's an invasion. I'm not used to being in the minority.

These little creatures must worship a fertility god. They are embarrassingly prolific. I believe in moderation in all things but they are as fertile as Iowa land. Their ability to fly gives them an unfair advantage. I believe in equality but only if I am more equal than you. I admit, I don't like you, little bug. You don't respect private property, namely mine.

I am big and strong, and you are little, tenacious, and unfairly persistent. I don't think you are an endangered species. Maybe I am.

Lines from the Left Behind
Snow Birds

This morning, the Canada geese are present in large numbers, despite our retirement facility's efforts to urge them to go elsewhere. They are on the bank of the lake, crossing the service road, and eating from our expensively maintained lawn. Oblivious to the humans who do not welcome them, they arrive in graceful formations, retract their landing gear, and make a safe and nearly splashless landing on our little lake. Some, who obviously have not read the book on Canada geese's habits, land on dry ground instead of on open water.

One goose walked across the road more slowly than the others, limping from a problem with its right leg. I wondered how this injury occurred. Maybe a turtle made an unwise decision and sank its teeth into a thin appendage underwater, only to discover that the large body above the water was not a good choice for a meal.

The morning parade has begun, with an orderly regiment of geese marching from the dining room lawn toward the southwest side of our building. The curve of the service road protects their parade ground and assembly area, though humans appear to be their only natural enemies. One laggard lingered to take a last drink from the lake before joining its companions.

Soon they will be gone. With no bags to pack and no flight plan to file, the geese will await some mysterious signal and lift off, form up in their great V, and be on their way. Their time in our lake and on our lawn has provided them with strength for their journey south. There they will winter in comfort, finding larger bodies of water on which to land and swim, as well as different grasses, berries, and delicacies to eat.

I am not one who assigns human thoughts and emotions to animals. I don't think Papa Canada Goose says to Mama Goose, "Gladys, we'll take off tomorrow. Do the kids know where we'll be?" Sometimes, though, when I see a goose flapping its large wings, I assume it is a male protecting his partner (wife) by a show of potential aggression toward an intruder. The two sexes, and I suppose there are two, exhibit behavior that seems remarkably human. You who love cats or dogs know what I mean. A book our discussion group is currently reading, *Water for Elephants*, goes rather far in this anthropomorphism in saying that Rosie, the circus elephant, smiles! Now really, that is too much.

Like the geese, our human snowbirds are preparing to escape the Iowa snow and ice. They light, stay a while, and fly away, unaware that they make the rest of us feel earthbound and dull. They have two residences, two sets of friends, two social lives, both more glamorous than the rest of us. Do they ever think of us when they're gone? Which place seems like home, or does either of them?

We who stay while our friends fly away, miss them. We miss eating with them, greeting them in the halls, chatting with them in the beauty shop. Committee meetings have some empty chairs; the book club loses their comments. On the other hand, we don't mind having less competition for the prize money on bingo night.

During the dark winter days, we will look forward to their return migration. We imagine that the beach sand felt good on their feet, whether webbed or not. Spring will bring them back to us. I share their pleasure in their leaving and look forward to their return. This is a time for all of us to do what keeps us energized and happy. We wish them all, human or avian, safe journeys. As the motel ad says, "We'll leave the light on for you."

Loving God,

We are here searching for a greater understanding and a more personal relationship with You.

We come quietly, tired from our busy day, but needing Your reassurance and comfort. Surround us with Your holy presence, we pray. Help us to gain strength from Your strength, compassion from Your love, and an increased understanding of our relationship to Your creation.

Help us to grow in our ability to discern what is real and true. We need Your enfolding and unending love as we live our lives.

Thank You for allowing us to remain useful in our lives, giving love and comfort to our families, friends, and those around us. We ask Your blessing.

Amen.

MUSINGS

Dreams

I killed a living creature this morning. It was only a spider, but it was functioning comfortably in its world. Its only sin was entering my world. I opened the door to my balcony and saw the little brown creature on the glass of the screen door. Was it inside or outside, I wondered. Unfortunately, it was inside. A rolled-up newspaper was my only weapon. At my first swat, the little creature dropped straight down and then scurried quickly to the bottom of the door. But not outside. "We cannot share this apartment. You must go," I announced. After a brief but unequal battle, the spider was dead. It was no longer a threat to my safety, which it never was.

Later I learned that my visitor (or invader) was of the order *Araneae*, an air-breathing arthropod with eight legs, four pairs of eyes, capable of emitting silk. Her evasive tactics were instinctive and perhaps my aggressive tactics were also. Spiders generally use elaborate courtship rituals to prevent the large females from eating the small males before fertilization, except where the male is so small he is not worth eating. This I did not need to know. Most spiders live for only one to two years. I hope my unwelcome visitor was nearing the end of her second year.

I could tolerate the spider on my balcony, admire her complex web, allow her to live her short life in peace. According to the scientists who study the connectedness of all energy, I am probably connected to that spider. I think it is a very distant relationship. Perhaps eventually I will be able to develop a sense of being a part of all creation. Not yet. I'm working on it.

◆

I have just paid a bill that I thought unreasonably high. I was more than annoyed. However, I wrote the check, addressed the envelope, put on a return address sticker, and reached for a stamp. To my dismay, my only stamp was one of those that should be used only for sending wedding invitations. It was a colorful confection that proclaimed LOVE across its front. Reluctantly I stuck the inappropriate stamp on the envelope while muttering, "I don't really mean it."

The Post Office should stay out of our personal relationships or at least show more restraint. Perhaps a pleasant little message like, "Have a nice day," or better yet, "I really don't like you very much," would do. Friends tell me that no one actually reads what stamps say, but I'm not so sure.

◆

Four pigeons have established squatters' rights on my balcony. Their personal habits may be quite acceptable by pigeon standards but disgusting to humans. The truly maddening thing about their behavior is their assumption of entitlement. "This is our place," they seemed to be saying.

I have exhausted my polite responses, of which I have a fairly short list when dealing with unwelcome feathered visitors. When I clap my hands and say very loudly, "Shoo!", they flip their tails in a most disrespectful way and continue to sit on the railing. Then I resort to threats. "If you don't leave, I'll call security and have you evicted." No response. "This is my balcony, you dirty birds, and I expect you to leave *now*," followed by another loud clap. More tail flipping and a slight change of position. "My guests can't sit on these chairs or walk on this floor," I say, hoping to appeal to their sense of guilt. "Too bad," their unruffled feathers say.

Perhaps I'm getting a little paranoid, but I fully expect them to have their own Facebook page. Sometime soon I'll read about this crazy old lady who thinks the balcony belongs to her when it is obviously theirs. "She couldn't possibly fly up that high," they'll write. I'll have to agree with that.

Just before my temper reaches a boiling point, some signal is received by the birds and they take off in loose formation. Perhaps they landed on your balcony. You just think it's yours.

◆ ◆ ◆

The other night I had a very vivid dream about my sister, seventeen years my senior, now dead many years. In my dream, I visited her and she showed me around her lovely home. She was obviously expecting another child. Her family life seemed idyllic. When I awoke, I remembered my dream and what had actually happened to her. She married her hometown sweetheart when he finished medical school and internship. He established a medical practice, began paying off his considerable school debts, and the couple welcomed a son. The year was 1940. My brother-in-law enlisted in the Army, although he would not have been drafted in World War II. Eventually, he was stationed outside London. My sister and their young son moved to our hometown and lived with our parents. Her husband never returned from the war. She never remarried.

I was married about the time of his death and thought I had no right to be happy because my sister was so devastated. I did not know then that relationships are not ended by life's tragedies or by death. Love shapes our lives forever and remains an enduring part of our thoughts and dreams.

◆ ◆ ◆

Perhaps it is the result of my standoff with the pigeons, but recently I have been thinking about indulging in drink. If wine bottles weren't so hard to open, I would drink more. Who designed them, my mother?

March 6, 2006

I have just marked my first anniversary as a householder in my hometown. It has been quite a year. There have been numerous trips from Des Moines to West Sunset Road to furnish my vacation house with items that would not fit into my apartment in the retirement facility. Each trip validated my decision to establish a part-time location in my hometown.

Much has changed in the small Iowa town over the years I have been gone. Most of my friends and family members are gone. My closest relative is now in his ninety-third year. I am of his generation, but a decade younger. The population has declined somewhat. Many people have left, but some others have moved to town, looking for a safe, welcoming place in which to raise a family or grow old close to family members. My Georgia-born husband and I came here briefly after WW II, but settled in the capital city. I remember how our three children loved visiting their grandparents and aunt. They could ride their bikes everywhere and go to the stores all by themselves.

Now I come alone, driving through the countryside, enjoying the changing views as the seasons change. Which season is the most beautiful? All of them together make up the tapestry of this lovely and fertile land. I watch for the wild creatures, the hawks, pheasants, and deer. Recently I saw eagles along the Raccoon River. Hawks are the easiest to spot, perched high on poles or trees. "Oh, there's one!" I exclaim to myself. I feel fortunate to see five or six hawks on my fifty-five mile trip.

I note the barns decorated with a barn quilt design. At first, I thought only newly painted barns should be adorned by these colorful patterns. Now I smile when I see a shabby barn sporting a bright quilt design. There is a certain bravery in showing vivid colors to the world even when your paint is peeling. I've bought several packets of note cards displaying the quilt designs. I'll send them to family and friends to let them know that Greene County is alive and well and flying its colors.

The Downtown Streetscape Vision is exciting. I want to be a shareholder in this plan for the town's future. All of the people who call it home should feel a sense of pride and ownership in this vision. Please include those of us who were once a part of this community in its future. We will always wish it success.

Late Summer Musings
July 2010

I'll try to enjoy this muggy, rainy season and not think of it as the beginning of a slide toward winter.

Blessings — My son has made numerous doctor-appointment runs for me in the past few weeks without complaining. He knows the questions to ask and can understand the answers. I must have done something right.

Speaking of slides, my body continues to function reasonably well, allowing me to join friends at dinner and dress up to attend Sip and Chat. The fragile social network here supports me.

My children and their assorted family members speak respectfully to and about me, at least within my hearing.

The uncertainty of life continues to surprise me in this retirement community, reminding me to enjoy each day and reach out to friends and neighbors with love.

My ex-daughter-in-law is visiting our family this weekend from her present home many miles away. I never think of her as an "ex." She is still my lovely daughter, if no longer my son's wife. Once you're attached to me, legally or otherwise, you're stuck forever.

This morning I lingered in my hot shower, standing longer than necessary for cleanliness. My Peace Corps granddaughter in Azerbaijan has no hot water in her Russian-built apartment. I wish I could share. She is helping the world and I am taking my luxuries for granted. Forgive me.

To Kiylah, at the opposite end of life's continuum. Eight months ago, I acquired an unexpected great-granddaughter. She was the result of a rebellious granddaughter's attachment to an opportunistic boy with only one thought in his empty head. I was not pleased. Now the baby looks at me with her big, bright eyes and smiles, showing her new teeth. "What would have happened to you in China, little unwanted female child?" I think. "You would probably have been left in an alley to starve or taken to an orphanage to be bought by rich Americans." Then I carefully lift her onto my lap and cuddle her sweet body. I hope we get to know each other before I am called to other duty.

Why would I share such intimate family news? I'm dismayed at my granddaughter's irresponsible behavior, but I'm not ashamed of this innocent baby. Please help me open hearts and welcome her into the human family.

My big farmer/cowboy son-in-law is raising unsprayed vegetables and fruit on his Iowa acres. "You're getting too green and pure for me," I tell him. Next year it is to be specially produced eggs from free-range hens. He will probably kill the old hens with painless injections. This progressive farmer says the yokes will be large and naturally yellow with the new feeding practices. I think sometimes progress means going back to old ways. Who knows? Big commercial farming seems to be the way of the future in Iowa. Is this a good thing? A thousand-acre farm was once a dream. Now it's a starter plot. A hundred bushels of corn to the acre? Double or triple that for success. I wonder if my father is getting crop bulletins in his final resting place. He would be amazed.

On the way to the store, I passed a man standing by a sign that said, "Unemployed." My husband worked hard to put food on our family's table. Is there food on that man's table? And I'm wasting food! My guilt level soars.

In my aisle walk at the grocery store, I looked at the amazing array of bottled drinks. One was labeled, "Dancing Bull." Can any Iowa person imagine a dancing bull? Bulls are unpredictable creatures, docile one moment, and trying to kill you the next. But dancing? Not likely. Instead of a strange drink, I bought a large can of baked beans, not because I wanted a large can but because it was two cents cheaper than the small can. I've given up trying to understand marketing.

On the fourth of July, my family was invited to a nearby lake home of my only sister's only son and his second wife. We sat inside, protected from the heavy rain, and ate abundant food, none of which I had prepared. I'm still invested in giving up guilt, but going to a potluck empty-handed is still a shameful thing. It was a pleasure to share a day with this not-so-young couple who have found such happiness the second time around. My sister, widowed in WWII, was an Aunty Mame character before the play was written. Her profession was teaching. She often took me with her on her summer travels. She showed me the world. I hope she is still spinning through the heavens saying, "Let's go! We still have lots to learn."

Recently I have been amusing myself by playing solitaire on the computer. It is a harmless waste of time, I tell myself. But is there such a thing when time is so precious? I'll ponder that tomorrow. Meanwhile, on with the games. Enjoy each day! Give up guilt.

Fall Musings
October 2010

There is a mischievous sprite that lives in my apartment. He exists to make my life more challenging, as though I need any more challenges. His last prank was to throw a favorite silver pendant far enough under my bed that I cannot see it nor reach it. I've tried using my cane as a tool for search and retrieval purposes, but without success. Next, I'll try to explain to one of the cleaning women what help I need. She will be embarrassed by her lack of understanding. Despite the welcome attempts by this facility to improve her language skills, she is still English-impaired, even more so when faced with new or unexpected requests. "Please retrieve my pendant from under the bed," will exceed her comprehension. I will resort to hand signals. I was not good at such games. She will be willing, eager to please, but mystified.

My granddaughter will come to visit this weekend and can understand my English better than I can understand hers. Her knees still bend without pain. The pendant that another granddaughter brought me from her semester abroad in Egypt will soon be safely back in my possession. Sunday brunch is a small price to pay for returning this precious (to me) little piece of jewelry. My resident sprite is probably still chuckling about his success in complicating my life. He doesn't know that I am amused at his little tricks.

◆

My son has a friend whose last name is Truthand. The man is a physician. His name is what intrigues and delights me. Imagine a doctor who always tells the truth AND. It is the "and" that I need. The truth, of course, but the "and" of kindness, compassion, and humility. He can give me his best judgment, the truth as he knows it, but also express concern for me, his patient. I am a willing but far from courageous fellow voyager on the perilous seas of life. Does anyone really know what the future holds? Perhaps a treatment has only a five percent success rate. If the research pool is large, five percent would be a lot of people. My friend, who has recently received a life-altering diagnosis, might be one of them. She has weathered serious health challenges before. She will probably jump into that pool and emerge as one of the five percent survivors. She needed the truth and compassion, delivered with kindness and respect, as we all do. My prayers are with her and all those who are in the same boat.

◆ ◆ ◆

Where are my buckeyes? When I recently checked the buckeye tree in the front yard of my little vacation house northwest of here, the current buckeye crop was almost ready to fall to the ground. When I visited the tree a few days ago, they had fallen. And disappeared! Only the rough outside shells remained of this once-a-year crop. I was mystified and angry. Who or what had made off with these delightful and ornamental nuts?

Searching for an explanation, I targeted the deer that climb the banks of the North Raccoon River to munch on the grasses, flowers and other plants in my neighborhood. Perhaps the foraging deer discovered this bounty and called their family members to a feast. Or perhaps the feasters were squirrels, or rabbits, or other of the many creatures who share living space with me.

I know very little about the eating habits of deer, so I decided to ask Yahoo! My question was, "Do deer eat buckeyes?" "Doubtful," responded Yahoo! "Buckeyes are poisonous to humans, cattle, and horses."

I don't want to accuse my neighbors. They watch my property and would not violate my privacy or ownership, even though I am present only occasionally. If some visitors to the area felt justified in harvesting these shiny nuts, I hope they enjoy their beauty, display them, but do not eat them. Buckeyes are known to bring good luck. I wish the feasters or harvesters had left a few more for me. I picked up fourteen by digging under the fallen leaves using the tip of my cane. Buckeyes keep well. I'll look forward to next year's crop, as all of us Iowans do.

◆

I didn't know what to expect after my recent soul-bruising revelation about my unexpected great-granddaughter. Would people still greet me in the halls, eat with me at dinner, smile as we meet? Or would they be judgmental, turn away, knowing but not understanding my guilt and embarrassment about my granddaughter's walk on the wild side?

Instead, they either said nothing, which I understood, or quietly confided that they too had a painful situation in their own family. Their kindness helped heal this deep wound and confirmed that this is a community of people working their way through life, doing the best they can, determined to love their neighbors even when they seem pretty unlovable or don't seem to deserve our love. Everyone needs and deserves love. Thank you.

When I look at this healthy and beautiful little girl, the old song creeps into my mind. "He's got the little bitty babies in His hands," and the words comfort me. We'll do what we can, control what we can, knowing that some things are not in our hands.

◆ ◆ ◆

Recently when I was out driving, I stopped at a stop sign. I waited for some time for the light to change. Don't laugh. If you haven't done something that foolish yet, you probably will.

Musings
January 2012

Perhaps this is no time to dwell on life's injustices, but if not now, when? Here are some of mine.

My investments keep decreasing and my waistline increases.

I work on downsizing my belongings and instead my apartment shrinks.

I have spent many hours in church over the years, and I'm still not perfect. Maybe in this New Year I'll figure things out.

◆ ◆ ◆

Here are some giving ideas for those of you who believe in the joy of giving even though you don't get a thank-you note. You remember that Nancy, my son-in-law's cow, is with calf. You might like to know that she is registered at the following stores:

Outsize Fashions in Guthrie Center for a moo-moo and other maternity wear for Nancy. Size E (for enormous).

Tinker's Bells in Jefferson for matching Swiss cow bells for the proud mother and her offspring.

Dairy Treats in Panora for cheese plates and other items for the lactose tolerant.

Boots, Shoes and FlipFlops in Rippey for MukLuks for mucking around in the barn lot. Two pairs for each, please.

Hope this has been helpful. Happy shopping.

◆ ◆ ◆

For many moons I have longed to see a "horse of another color."* I imagined a truly fabulous array of colors, never seen in our mundane world. Recently, on a trip to Colorado to visit my son and daughter-in-law, I had just that experience.

Their house is southwest of Denver in the foothills. After much turning and climbing from the Denver airport, we turned into their unsurfaced lane. Trees surrounded us—evergreen, poplar, spruce, birch, and aspen—though I could not have named them at that time. The lane was long and curved but eventually ended in a clearing before a multi-level house. The air was brisk, but firewood stacked on the deck near the entrance to the house suggested colder weather to come. "We are at 8,650 feet above sea level," my son informed me.

"Foothills indeed," I thought. "We're in the mountains. I wonder if I can breathe up this high."

We entered the house on the middle level, walking into a large open space of entrance hall, living room, dining area, and open kitchen. From that level, one could see the upstairs with an open balcony, a corner seating area, crammed bookshelves, bathroom, and doors to two bedrooms. A stairway led down to a lower level. I was hardly inside the front door before I saw my dream horse. She stood on four wooden legs that ended in elegant hooves. Feathers decorated with crystal beads circled the ankles. The graceful body, neck, and head were covered in a spotted brown-and-white material, soft to the touch. The top of her head was about chest high to me. Mane and tail were real feathers of browns, russets, and tans, perhaps wild turkey, pheasant, even owl. Long silver strands of beads hung from her ears. Her head was slender with a Thoroughbred's air of arrogance. She most resembled a Paint horse but of a unique pattern. Exquisite.

The next morning, sunshine filled the rooms, entering through tall windows on three sides of the main area. To the west, a mountain with snow on its top reminded me that I was truly in the high foothills and the real mountains were not far away. Even this gorgeous view could not detract from my delight in the little horse. I later learned that she was a product of the imagination of a local artist in the area of Conifer, Colorado. If I had trouble breathing, it was from the beauty of the home and its surroundings, not from the thin mountain air.

* "Horse of another color" is an old saying that means "something entirely different."

◆ ◆ ◆

Frankly, I am a little impatient with our advertisements that extoll the virtues of our retirement community to anyone of retirement age. I'm ready to set some requirements for living at Deerfield. Why shouldn't people apply to live here? Here are some ideas for an application form.

___ Have you lived a pretty stable life, paid your bills on time, put some money aside, tried to love your neighbors, made a few mistakes, regretted them, and apologized?

___ Do you have any talents you could share? Do you play a musical instrument? Did you ever sing in a chorus? Do you enjoy listening to music?

___ Have you enjoyed traveling, but now want shorter and well-planned trips? (We recently toured the World Food Prize Hall of Laureates in downtown Des Moines. Ambassador Kenneth Quinn, President of the World Food Prize Foundation, told us the stories behind this amazing Iowa gem.)

___ Have many of your friends moved away? Do you need some new partners for bridge or other of your favorite games? Are you open to making new friends? (That will be easy to do.)

___ You seldom wear tattered jeans and never to dinner. (We do have some standards, but not for grandchildren.)

___ You may have taken some risks in your younger days, but now you want a sure thing.

If you checked even one of these requirements, you qualify. You're ready for us, and we're ready to welcome you. Don't wait too long. Come while you can enjoy all that Deerfield offers.

Musings
February 2012

Memories can come swiftly and disappear just as suddenly. Some, however, remain a permanent part of our consciousness. When I think of my early school years, fifth or sixth grade, I sense a clear picture of a recess game. This was a time when boys and girls played together on the playground, without giggling, showing off, or dividing into cliques. The game I remember was called Robin Hood, based on our limited knowledge of the long-ago resident of Sherwood Forest. Advantages of the game were that almost any number could play and there was always an opposing force trying to capture the heroic Robin Hood and his men. Another advantage was that his followers were not all male. Girls could live in the forest, shoot bows and arrows with amazing accuracy, and lead the dreaded Sheriff of Nottingham away from Robin's forest hideaway.

Of all who ran through the forest, none was faster than Robin Hood and his good friend, Maid Marian. In my memory, I was always Maid Marian. I felt the wind in my hair and ground under my feet as I outpaced everyone except Robin. The wicked Sheriff never caught us. We continued to rob the rich and give to the poor. Only the school bell-ending recess stopped this wonderful childish drama. But it hasn't stopped. I can still feel my hair blowing, my legs pounding, and the thrill of the chase.

Robin Hood grew up, went to Drake University Law School, and became a judge, still fighting evil perhaps. My running days are long past. The memory of them remains. I feel blessed.

• ◆ •

A dinner companion related a memory from her childhood. Her parents took her into Chicago to her music lesson when she was too young to walk from the station. Her mother stayed with her during the lessons, but her father used that time to buy tickets to Broadway musicals. When she plays that wonderful music, she relives the experience of seeing the shows with her parents. These memories are unfading for her, a bright ribbon of pleasure across the years.

• ◆ •

A much sadder memory has recently been revealed in the book by Mimi Alford called *Once Upon a Secret*. Now seventy years old, Mrs. Alford writes of an eighteen-month period of her life when she and President John F. Kennedy had a continuing sexual affair. She was nineteen and still in school when it began. She was hired as an intern in the White House, a position for which she had not applied. The tawdry events started on her fourth day in that job when she was invited to go swimming in the White House pool, which she had not even known existed.

What are we to make of the events Mrs. Alford relates in her book? They describe the handsome, powerful, much older man deliberately selecting the naïve young girl as his ongoing sexual partner. He was the President of the United States, married, respected, the leader of the free world! The risk was enormous; the rewards were brief, transitory, and sordid.

Many of our questions about the relationship between the terribly unequal couple are answered in Mrs. Alford's carefully detailed account of it. She described in painful and horrifying detail what happened to her as a naïve schoolgirl. Although she did not perceive it as such, this first encounter was a sexual assault. The President took her on a tour of the White House, then into a bedroom (actually Jackie's) where he lowered her to the bed and "took my virginity." Nothing in her protected background prepared her to handle such an unimaginable situation. She didn't say "No." When he asked if she was all right, she replied that she was. What a mixture of emotions she must have felt—amazement, excitement, disbelief, embarrassment. Judge her if you must, but with compassion.

The President sometimes sent a limousine to her college to bring her to the White House for their trysts. Sometimes she traveled with the President's party to events in other cities or states, often waiting in a hotel room until he could join her. Even now, after more than fifty years of keeping this immense secret, she could not blame him. She still thinks he cared for her. In an interview, she spoke of "unburdening" herself by writing this book. She tries to understand his motivation and says only that there was something "lacking" in him and that he was "so needy." She observed that he could compartmentalize his life and his emotions. Did he have so little concern for the enormous responsibilities he had to the country as well as to his wife and extended family? This question and others will never be answered, at least to my satisfaction.

◆ ◆ ◆

In my continuing effort to protect all of us from various illnesses and other challenges, I have found some new ones to warn you about. Here they are:

Alektorophobia – fear of chickens (probably not a major danger here).

Coulrophobia – fear of clowns. (My daughter suffers from this one. I knew I shouldn't have let her brother wear that clown suit on Halloween when they were little.)

Neophobia – fear of new things (obviously quite widespread here).

Pentheraphobia – fear of one's mother-in-law. (I'll check with my son-in-law.)

◆ ◆ ◆

Sometimes memory fails us. Recently I put a teakettle of water on the stove, turned on the burner, and returned to my TV program. When I returned much later, the water had boiled away and parts of the teakettle had melted. I had heard no warning sounds, smelled no evidence of burning. I am well aware of what could have resulted from this memory lapse. I share this incident with you as a reminder that our memory is sometimes undependable. Being extra cautious is the right thing to do. I will replace the damaged teakettle but make every effort to remember what caused the damage.

◆ ◆ ◆

If you will share your memories with me, I promise not to reveal that you liked Elvis Presley's moves more than his music. Make some new, happy memories and enjoy!

Musings
March 2012

I enjoy hearing the memories of my dinner companions. They remember their school years as happy times, even the bitterly cold winters. Now our current mild winter is over. Welcome spring!

◆ ◆ ◆

Many things can trigger a memory, including pain. Without warning, sometimes I get slammed with a sharp pain over my heart. My breath catches, my speech stops, my body concentrates on surviving this unexplained invasion. Then in a few minutes, it is gone. I have described these events to my doctor. He wants to be present when one happens. It doesn't work that way, I tell him. "What does it feel like?" he asks. Immediately I flash back to high school when I had pleurisy complete with similar sharp, stabbing pains.

I was in high school when pleurisy struck. More important than missed classes were missed play practices. That I could not accept. Before my body was ready, I returned to the school stage to learn my lines and prepare for the big performance. Half the town would be there. Some of my friends knew of my struggle to perform and to ignore the pain. One of those friends was a fellow actor, a boy who was not usually found on the stage. He was the high school football star, a small (by today's standards), wiry player who led the team with speed and cleverness. An average student in the classroom, he was a standout on the athletic field.

I was intrigued by his athletic ability, which I did not possess, and by his assurance in any physical contest. I yelled for him along with the students, parents, and townspeople. He made our Friday nights exciting. Friday nights he was a hero. A shy, studious sixteen year old, I had little knowledge of teenaged boys. To be honest, I was more than a little afraid of him. Only on stage did we communicate comfortably. I wanted him to like me. What would he think of me if I grabbed my chest and couldn't say my lines? I would soon find out.

During a play practice, the pleurisy pain hit hard. I was aware of his reaction. It was somewhere between fear and horror. "Hey, let me help you," he said. "I'll get Mrs. Jacquis." (She was a favorite teacher and mother of two of our classmates.) "She'll know what to do."

Of course, I let him help me. The play went off smoothly, and I knew I had seen a side of him that few people had. We went our separate ways, to different colleges. World War II took over our world. He became a colonel in the Army Air Force flying fighter planes and stayed in the service for twenty years. He retired to a cattle ranch in southern Missouri, a husband, father, and grandfather. We kept in touch through our class newsletter and danced a few times at class reunions. He and his wife divorced and he moved to Texas, where he remarried. We were still friends. To me, he was a hero with a kind heart who flew fast planes for his country, played tough football for our little town, and helped a scared young girl. My pain reminds me of a longtime friend and his unexpected gentleness.

◆

Our memories of frigid winters make our first spring sightings especially delightful. Again we are blessed with these special signs. Daylight Savings Time caught us unawares, but we have sprung forward as instructed. Now it is dark when we awaken, but light as we eat dinner. The trees along the road to the main entrance are sprouting reddish buds. Crocuses, grape hyacinths, and tulips have made an early appearance above the awakening soil. Grass is changing from tan to green in spots, to the delight of our flock of Canada Geese. We residents open our balcony doors on these seventy-degree afternoons and wonder if we will pay for these warm days later.

Marge Koester says that we are missing some of the sights and sounds of spring if we are not aware of the birds that are returning or passing through our area. "Get outdoors," she urges. "Look, listen, be patient. You will be amazed at the variety of wild life you will see." For those of us who need guidance, Marge lists the birds that we may see.

First, the robins are colorful and noisy, the male flaunting his red breast and announcing his territory with his distinctive call. Look quickly and you will see the many warblers preparing for the nesting season.

Larger birds are with us also. More bald eagles are visible than in some former years, soaring gracefully above us or roosting motionless high in the trees. Not so handsome but necessary for clearing woods, highways, and fields of carrion are the turkey vultures, ugly on the ground but graceful in flight. The Canada geese are seen in pairs now, with the male aggressively chasing off any bachelors approaching his mate.

Some visitors rest briefly in our area on their journeys north. The huge white pelicans with wingspreads up to eight feet sometime stop over for a few days. The great egret and the great blue heron have been seen on our pond in former years. Perhaps they will visit us again this year.

Ducks also light here. Marge has seen wood duck, mallard, blue-winged teal, shoveler, and scaup on our pond in past years. Currently, she is expecting to see the goldfinch changing to its bright yellow coat. She has heard owls but not yet seen any. Owls are difficult to see but occasionally can be heard. The large barred owl with its brown eyes may be heard in daytime, but is a nocturnal bird. Soon Marge and Mary Slantz will clean the bluebird houses so those lovely little birds will have an inviting place to nest.

Remember the seven "s" words to identify birds. They are: song, size, shape, situation (surroundings), shading, sweep, and seasons. Spring is a wonderful season to observe, identify, and enjoy birds. Marge will be delighted if you let her know what you see. Relax and enjoy!

◆ ◆ ◆

Announcement! My son-in-law's Jersey cow, Nancy, delivered her offspring on March 11, a black, half-Angus male calf. A sure sign of spring! Mother and baby are doing just fine.

Musings
April 2012

My dinner companions often share their memories, happy and sad. Recently one woman told of being disappointed by the lack of appreciation for her efforts to write a family history and share it at a family reunion. "I even took a class in how to write my memoirs. It took me months to do the project. Then I made a copy for everyone who would be at the reunion." Irritation was apparent in her voice. "Do you know what happened? Nobody cared. They put the book back on the table and continued visiting. They never even read it! I was so hurt." She is still hurt after all these years.

I'm pleased to say that no one told her she "shouldn't" feel that way, it was a long time ago, and she "should" just move on. We know that not all memories are happy ones, but they are part of our lives. Is it ever too late to make amends for actions that hurt others? Perhaps we should try.

◆ ◆ ◆

At church recently, one of our ministers asked the congregation, "What do you pray for?" Perhaps good health, she suggested, or the safety and well being of those we love, even world peace. Then she said, "At the heart of all these prayers is one cry: God, make me happy. We're not that different from the disciples in the boat. (Mark 8:31-39) For generations, people had been lamenting to God: Save us. Save us from our pain. Save us from oppression. Save us. Make us happy."

She continued, "We say we want to be happy, but when we get a glimpse of what it might require of us — how we might need to change how we spend our time or our money or change how we talk to and treat others or maybe even ourselves — well. Surely there's a way to be happy and keep doing what we're doing, right?"

It was a good sermon, one I continued to think about long after the service was over. I did not, however, remember ever praying specifically for happiness. I don't think people of my generation do. We've lived too long. We tend to be realistic people, accepting of the ups and downs of life. To pray to God to make us happy seems foolish, trivial. Better to ask for strength to deal with whatever comes. Your will, not mine. To pray that God will make us happy. I don't think so.

◆ ◆ ◆

A small gesture of kindness made me happy recently. The Spiritual/Emotional team of FitSix has started giving a gift bag with a thoughtful note and a cookie to various residents. It is a way of expressing friendship and caring. I recently found one of those little gift bags on my front door handle. What a delightful surprise! I don't need to pray to God to make me happy. Human kindness will do just fine.

◆ ◆ ◆

Two by two by two, the Canada geese clamber up the grassy slope from the pond. Two by two by two, they eat their fill of the newly green grass. Then suddenly a raucous sound and flapping of great wings break the silence. An interloper has come too close to one pair of geese and is strongly challenged by the male goose. "Don't come any closer to my mate," he warns.

Giving chase, he forces the intruder to retreat. It is a ritual dance of challenge and response, an age-old expression of protection for a mate. Such has been the way of the bird world long before we bird watchers were aware of it. Soon there will be little goslings swimming in a line, guarded by one parent in front and one behind. How fortunate we are to have front-row seats to this drama.

◆ ◆ ◆

While rearranging flowers this morning, I found I was down to four blooms from two large bouquets. It's strange how some flowers last so much longer than others. That seems to be true of people too. Those of us living here together are among the hardier blooms. Making friends and staying active are part of the secret to living life fully.

Income Tax Rant

This was going to be my annual income tax rant. I do not rant easily. It is not my style. This year, however, I intend to make my feelings known. I do not think the governments, state and federal, use my money well. The administrators divert too much into their own pockets through exorbitant salaries, funding projects that do not improve the lives of the people they are supposed to serve, and by actual dishonesty of reporting and sleight-of-hand budgeting.

My personal income is modest, mostly the result of years of working, saving, and investing. My husband and I managed money differently; he looked long term, and I provided for more immediate needs and pleasures. Our family rocked along comfortably, guided by his frugality motivated by memories of the Great Depression, and my feelings of security from my Iowa farm background. We always had what we needed, although few luxuries. The children benefited from my willingness to support some of their wishes. I am living now in what many would consider luxury because of my husband's careful investing. I wish he had had more time and health to enjoy it.

Back to my rant. Next month I will write checks for thousands of dollars to people I don't know, government entities I don't trust, for funding programs I think are failing. I have the right to support candidates of either of two parties, both of which have disappointed me. What do I really know about any of these candidates? I doubt my perceptions of their honesty and their desire to represent me fairly. I remember that I was quite impressed with the smooth-talking and handsome John Edwards. I couldn't have been more wrong about him. One of his greatest Iowa supporters was Roxanne Conlin, the bright and ambitious trial lawyer who ran for the United States Senate. If she could be fooled, perhaps it was not so strange that I fell under his spell.

The new health care bill is touted as the best thing the government has accomplished or lambasted as the worst. It probably is neither, but I don't know. Those people who speak for or against it probably don't know either. They would like us to think they do, but my years in higher education convince me they haven't read or understood this massive bill. I am quite sure it will cost us all a great deal of money and generate new opportunities for greed, deception, and fraud.

My desire to rant is declining, along with my energy. Perhaps I am exhausted by all the reasons to be angry and the equally good reasons to step back and hope. After all, in the future more people should be able to have health insurance coverage, which is a good thing. Medicare will probably continue to subsidize my health coverage and yours. Some of my tax dollars will hopefully provide goods and services that are desperately needed. Newspapers will continue to uncover and publicize the failures of individuals and groups, seldom the successes. You and I still have a voice and a vote and the responsibility that every citizen has to participate in the workings of this wonderful country. Only dictators have total control and usually not for long.

In lieu of an exhausting and probably useless rant, I am going to look for ways to enjoy my life now. I plan to:

Participate in the activities I enjoy and not feel guilty about avoiding others;

Eat with various people and become better acquainted with them;

Visit friends in the Health Center and try to brighten their day;

Write thank you notes for kindnesses people have done for me;

Forget some of the rigid rules of behavior I grew up with;

Remember that many of the "good old days" were not so great;

Read a book that takes me to a different culture and try to understand it;

Invite a grandchild to the Sunday brunch;

Give to Iowa Public Television;

Talk twice as much about the future as about the past.

Maybe some of these activities will lift my gloom. Of course, I will still have to write those checks. But then, so will you. Have a good day anyway.

Musings
May 2012

I want to nominate the Austrian billionaire for the award of "Optimist of All Time." If there isn't such an award, there should be. He recently remarried at the age of 94, saying that he wanted more children. The reporter of this story felt that he may have been joking, but who knows? His adult children are not amused. However, money can buy many things.

◆

We have rules here that sometimes need an explanation. One of them is the rule against taking food out of the dining room. This does not apply to the neatly packaged food in the large white sacks. It relates to the food that you ordered for your meal and didn't consume in the dining room. There is evidently a state regulation against recycling this food to our refrigerators for use in a future lunch. The state regards us as a vulnerable population and we must be protected. Put kindly, we may or may not remember to use leftover food before it spoils.

This is probably a good rule, so put away your little plastic bags and stop thinking what a good sandwich that piece of ham or slice of roast beef would make.

◆

I think it is time to update you on the growth and behavior of Nancy's calf. He is still quite young but his growth is well within expectations. He is now probably slightly larger than Marian's dog, Winston. Since he is of mixed breed, his color is close to that of his Black Angus father (an absentee parent), but mixed with the golden shade of his Jersey mother. A handsome young bull, most would agree. Despite some comments that I have "milked" this story far too long, I shall continue.

It is his behavior that disappoints me. My son-in-law recently reported that Curley is not gamboling in the nearby meadow as I had expected. He is physically capable of such activity, but is either uninterested in running and jumping or hasn't yet learned what young animals do. There are no other calves his age to play with on the farm. His mother is a phlegmatic creature, a truly boring bovine, who keeps her son close to her side. There is a miniature horse of evil disposition, appropriately named Diablo, but the young bull is better off far away from him. Three adult riding horses do not qualify as playmates. Curley may have spotted the red fox running through the pasture, but discarded the idea of trying to keep up with that swift creature.

I am currently looking for a day care center for calves where he could learn the joys of active play. I believe all young creatures must be socialized and taught to play well with others. My children went to an excellent church-sponsored nursery school that tried to teach aggressive youngsters to be less so and vice versa. Biting was frowned upon and hitting was not encouraged. This was where I first learned about time-outs but preferred taking them myself.

The somewhat liberal and permissive school was quite successful except in the case of one particularly stubborn little girl. She was sent home the last day of the school term for enthusiastically punching another child in the stomach. My children grew into model citizens, two aggressive lawyers, and one successful businessman who does not always play well with others. Biting and hitting, however, are still not allowed.

I am aware that many of you frown on naming animals. "Anthropomorphic," you sniff. You would be right. However, if you see a big cowboy-looking guy in the dining room, you may not want to tell him that he can't name his animals.

♦ ◆ ♦

Here are some ways we can honor our dear Marian:

See the world as a glass half full. Treat each other kindly. Enjoy dressing up and looking ridiculous. Never say we're too old to do something interesting. Look for new solutions to old concerns. Be loyal. See good in everyone. Keep moving. Think outside the box. Value creativity. Eat no meat for a day or two. Wear bright colors and youthful fashions, and establish your own style. Have fun with clothes and life. Visualize her running along the Lake Michigan shoreline leading, or being led, by her enormous dog.

Be happy for her in her new stage of life. Grandmothering is great! She left us a wonderful legacy. Treasure it.

Marian helped make Deerfield the place it is, where kindness is contagious. She was our sparkplug and our heart. Many happy years to you, Marian. Don't forget us.

◆ ◆ ◆

This morning I saw a bluebird fly from its nesting box to the top of a young tree nearby. What a great sight to start the day!

◆ ◆ ◆

France recently celebrated Joan of Arc's 600th birthday, and you think you're old. Let's celebrate each one of our years.

Lines from My Retirement Home

I've grown accustomed to lines. They are a major part of my life at this retirement facility, as at all such places. Like well-behaved schoolchildren, my friends and I line up to enter the bus and then reverse the process when we reach our destination. We line up to be seated in the dining room, line up for treats at our many meetings, and line up to be seated in our too-small living room.

Recently, we lined up for the bus ride to the Civic Center to attend the Symphony. The soaring music lifted our spirits but reminded us of other concerts which we attended with family members. Then there was an arm to hold or a hand to squeeze. We never envisioned a life when we would be alone.

We are grateful for the convenience of being delivered to the door and helped carefully down the steps. We mourn the freedom of driving ourselves and walking easily from the parking ramp to the concert venue. We waited in line to exit with all the other drivers, but somehow that wait did not diminish our spirit, just our patience.

We live with lines. There are the lines in our faces, the lines we learn to say when asked how we are. "Just fine," we answer, a true response. We're grateful for the comfort, the safety, the services. Do we like living here? As compared with our own homes with family around us? That's not the question and we have learned our line well.

We serve on committees that have no real purpose. They are advisory, we're told. Does anyone listen to our advice? What difference do our years of experience make? "Your ideas are very valuable to us," the leaders say, but we suspect that we are being fed just another line.

We wonder about our neighbors who suddenly disappear. "Where is Mary and how is she?" "We can't tell you anything," we're told. "The privacy law, you know." Another line, true in its bureaucratic meaning, but unkind in its lack of humanity.

We watch the Dow in its unfathomable ups and downs. How will our little pot of investments fare in this turbulence? Our children reassure us. "You don't have anything to worry about, Mother. You'll be fine." Fine! We've seen hard times before, and we know what depression and a stock market crash means. We remember banks closing and people standing in soup lines. We do not have time to wait for the long haul, for the inevitable recovery. Our children are kind. We will accept their well-meaning line.

Let us absolve the politicians for their guilt in feeding us their party lines. We listen to their promises of change (to what?) and problems solved without cost to us, the taxpayers. More and more will be provided without new taxes in this broken economy. Who said we had to swallow all their lines?

In my future, and I don't really mind thinking about it, I will join another line. I will move gently into strange territory, and yet it will seem familiar and welcoming. I imagine crossing a wide river and going easily up a hill to a city of light. Enormous gates will open as I approach. And there will be—another line. At least I know what will be at the end of that line. It will be worth waiting for.

Want and Need

This is a tale of want and need, those two four-letter words that get us into so much trouble. I don't want or need a different car. My present car sits comfortably in the east garage amid makes and models both older and newer, of greater and lesser value, and perhaps even higher mileage. It is comfortable and dependable, until something unexpected goes wrong. It has gotten me in and out of the tricky main entrance without a scratch, at least up to this point. We have an unspoken agreement. I take care of the car, and it takes me in comfort and safety wherever I want to go. We are growing old together. I show my age more than it does and have many more miles on me, though they are not so visibly recorded. I expected to end my driving years with this car.

My daughter wants to purchase a different car for me. Not pay for it, you understand, just do the fun parts. These include search on the Internet for just the right make, model, color, year — all the things that excite her and confuse me. The real fun for her is the negotiation on price. Not my cup of tea.

I have done my share of negotiations. What woman hasn't? The item of my desire, however, was never a car. Now a lovely piece of jewelry, that is worth intense negotiation. That brings the adrenaline rush, the flush to the cheeks, the sweaty palms, the shallow breathing. Jewelry is an affectation, a non-essential part of one's wardrobe, an escape from life's realities. I love it.

My most recent venture into the rarified atmosphere of want involved a string of beads. Not just any beads, but a single strand of matched Tahitian pearls, black with a lovely sheen that would make anyone's complexion glow. They carried a price that assured me they were genuine. The clerk in the jewelry shop had noticed me drooling on the display case and identified me as a live prospect. I'm sure she saw that the pearls would last much longer than I would, but that is one of the advantages of jewelry. I have granddaughters who would eventually appreciate them.

A purchase of pearls was not one to be made lightly or in only one visit. Gathering my dignity around me, I said that I would keep them in mind. In mind! How could I forget them? I made it successfully to the door, opened it reluctantly, and escaped. In some foreign countries I have visited, the shopkeeper would have followed me outside, saying, "You like? How much you pay?" Since this was the United States, we played a different game. The clerk knew I would be back another day. Perhaps then we would come to a courteous and low-key agreement.

What do the pearls have to do with a new car? Neither falls into the "need" category. What a dilemma! The sensible decision would be to dismiss both of them from my thoughts. Not easily done. My children say that I should get what I want. They are probably not thinking about these items. Did I choose either? I'll let you know when I decide.

Musings on a Blah Day

While fixing my breakfast recently, I admitted that I didn't feel very well. Nothing really new. No excruciating pain, no deep cough, no chills and fever. Just a feeling of absence of energy and a lack of desire to start the day. The coffee didn't smell inviting, the breakfast food bored me, and there was no sweet roll to top off the meal.

Since no one was going to fix my world for me, I thought of some things I could do to make myself feel better. Here are some ideas that occurred to me. Perhaps they might work for you too.

Write a poem and don't judge it.
Watch a silly TV show.
Write a note to a friend.
Perform a random act of kindness.
Talk back to an irritating ad on TV.
Sing to yourself.
Practice meditating.
Count your blessings.
Forgive anyone who has hurt you.
Forgive yourself.
Ignore advice that doesn't feel right, including this.
Have a good day, and I will too!

COURAGE

Courage and Hope

Examples of courage are everywhere. How we admire the Staff Sgt. from Hiawatha, Iowa, who recently was awarded the Medal of Honor for his valor while in the service. Or the little girl who walked through the snow and bitter cold to get help for her mother and baby brother when their car slid off the road. We were amazed at the bravery of the protestors in Egypt and Libya who risked their lives to force tyrants to give up their power and leave the countries.

We can be proud of these people without really understanding their actions or motivations. Their actions went far beyond the everyday acts of courage that we understand. Our own daily acts of courage will never garner us a Medal of Honor, nor would we expect them to. In fact, most of us don't recognize them ourselves. They seem routine, insignificant. They just come with the territory of life.

Small acts of courage surround us. Often we overlook them or take them for granted. Here are some small, or not so small, acts of courage we see every day.

The courage to keep watch in the sick room with a suffering spouse.

To return to the dining room after the death of a loved one and to accept the fact that life goes on without him or her.

To get out of bed in the morning when every part of your body aches.

To be kind and loving to a grandchild who has violated all the rules the family lives by.

To say to the doctor, "Tell me the truth. I can handle it."

The courage to say to another resident, "What can I do to help you?"

Such little things! Such beautiful, loving actions!

Where does this homely, everyday courage come from? From our parents, from habit, early training, or from Grace? Does it spring from our religious beliefs or the deep hope that what we have been taught is true?

Scriptures tell us that we are safe, we are all right. They reassure us with hopeful messages. "There is a light of the world, a kingdom of heaven inside us that will bear us up, regardless of our sorrow, fear, or loss. The kingdom of God is already here. It is within us and among us."

We have been given the courage to greet the day with a smile when everything seems hopeless. Courage generates hope. We see it around us every day and each of us contributes to it.

"Surely, goodness and mercy will follow me all the days of my life." That is the promise. Live it hopefully and courageously. Against all evidence, I still hope. So do you.

You do it every day.

God bless.

Fear or Fear Not

Recently I was sitting with friends at dinner when the talk turned to travel. Each person said she would not travel overseas again because it was too dangerous. "You never know where the next terrorist attack will happen. Look at that awful event in Mumbai. Hundreds were killed. And the riots in Egypt. Terrifying!"

"I used to like cruises," another woman said, "but now there are pirates attacking cruise ships. I won't take a chance on a cruise ever again."

"You have to fly to board a ship," a third woman commented. "Flying has become too dangerous. I don't intend to fly anywhere, not even to visit my son and his family in Boston. Now that's a dangerous city, too."

"I loved train trips," the first woman said. "I won't travel by train anymore. I've heard about luggage being stolen and even some passengers being mugged. I'll just stay here."

Later as I was thinking about our conversation, I felt depressed. All of these women had led full and active lives. They had traveled, taken risks, enjoyed visiting family and friends, visited many states and countries. But those days were past, they said. Travel was too uncomfortable, uncertain, and dangerous. What was different, I wondered, the world or our perception of it? When we downsized our households to move to a retirement community, had we also downsized our world? Is the world truly so dangerous now that we must retreat into an ever-smaller corner and never venture out?

Perhaps it is that dangerous. We watch the news and see incredible events that take innocent lives. We see actual scenes of war with people killed and maimed before our eyes. We see planes flown into huge buildings, killing thousands. We see tidal waves that sweep enormous numbers of people to their deaths. Is the world a dangerous place? Of course it is.

I tried to put this perception of a dangerous world out of my mind, but it kept coming back to me. Was our world really so much more dangerous today than it was when we were younger? Were we feeling a new dimension of fear today? What was its source and how could we protect ourselves from it?

The world my husband and I faced when we moved to Des Moines in 1946 after World War II was a pretty scary place. We had no money and no job. We knew almost no one. We came anyway, perhaps with the courage of youth, but more likely the naïve assumption that we would find a job and a place to live, and things would turn out all right. We started our civilian married life on faith (in ourselves), hope (in a world in which hard work and good intentions would be rewarded), and charity (handouts of food from my parents). Love was present too.

Perhaps we were afraid, but I don't remember that we were. Thousands of other young couples were in the same situation. Many families were trying to establish a "normal" life, in cities or small towns, some on farms, most with help from their extended families. Eventually my husband found a job and we were able to buy a home, actually a duplex, after borrowing the money for the down payment. In time, we experienced the blessing of children.

I remember trying to teach the children, two boys and a little sister, how to deal with the world as I knew it. "You must be big and strong, tough and brave," I said. They knew they were not big and strong and had no idea how to be tough and brave. I sent them to a camp south of Des Moines where they were taught to ride horses. The boys tolerated the camp, but little sister hated it. She was terrified of the gentle horse she was supposed to ride. "He's so big, Mother. I'm scared I'll fall off," she wept. Finally, she got on, hung on, and didn't fall off.

The boys were two years apart in age, so shared the same Cub Scouts and Boy Scouts activities. One night they were on an overnight campout when a summer storm blew up with heavy rain, wind, and lightning. I was terrified. I insisted that my husband drive out to the camp and bring the boys home so they'd be safe.

It took some persuading, but eventually he backed the station wagon out of the garage and headed for the camp. I was sure lightning would strike the camp or his car, probably both. After an eternity, the station wagon came back up the drive and into the garage. Dashing to the door, I waited for my husband and sons to come into the safe, warm house. My husband came in—alone!

"Where are they?" I exploded, fear pouring from every cell of my body.

"Oh, they were fine. Their tent was pretty dry, so I left them there. They didn't even know I checked on them." their father replied. I remember being relieved, grateful, and furious with him. My boys were learning to be big and strong, tough and brave. I still had some lessons to learn.

What could I say now to my friends who were so fearful? Is there a time for bravery and a time to avoid risk, I wondered. Or is risk as necessary to a full life as breathing? Who can say that it is wrong to avoid the things we fear, if we can? Carefully we draw the boundaries of our lives tighter and tighter. Surely then, we will not feel fear.

But we do. Fear creeps in, disturbing our sleep, invading our dreams, clouding our vision, making us say, "I can't. I won't. No. No." If our dear children want to see us, they must come to us because we won't fly or ride the train and certainly not drive. We miss them, but the journey is too dangerous. Fear rises up around us, encircling us with terrible images of disaster. We are imprisoned in an ever-smaller room of imagined safety. We don't notice that there are bars on the windows of this tiny room.

The women at the table were right. We are right to be cautious, to watch where we step, to give up the car keys when we're unsure about driving, to be sensible about all of our life choices. And yet, I kept hearing some familiar words from my childhood. "Fear not," I heard in my mind. "Fear not."

Was this a message I needed to hear? When fear sits on my shoulder and says, "You can't," I'll remember those words. Fear will not control my life. There is still much joy in the world for each of us if we live each day to the fullest. I will tell myself, "Fear not, for I am with you. All is well. All is well indeed."

HOPE

Out of the Fog
Lines on a Foggy Day

This morning I opened my living room blinds to greet the day. I looked southwest toward our lake and it was gone. A low, gray fog had silently covered the lake, the lawn, the grasses, and the bike path. Also gone were the houses in the distance. The park area between our retirement facility and the family homes had also disappeared. My familiar view was totally changed. The world outside my window was soft and gray and blank. The fountain in the lake must still be splashing away, but I can't see it or hear it. It has to be there, doesn't it, I thought.

What can I believe about a world that can disappear overnight? Sometimes I think my grasp on reality is a little shaky. This strange gray world confirms my fears. Yesterday I watched a young man jogging on the bike path, a mother holding her dog's leash while pushing her baby's carriage. I anticipated the East Indian woman's morning walk along the security road and over to the bike path. Her traditional trousers and long tunic, usually orange, made a delightful splash of color. Where are these people who were dependable figures in my world yesterday? Have they left or have I?

We all know that our world can change without warning. Sometimes it happens suddenly, when a son dies and leaves his young family. Sometimes it is slower, when the brain forgets its functions and the body no longer responds. Words disappear from our tongues and memories retreat in a confusing fog.

My husband was a Navy pilot in WWII. When the neurologist tested him to chart his descent into Alzheimer's, he couldn't remember the word "helicopter." The picture was familiar; the name of that flying object was gone. Gone where, gone how? He did not know, nor did I.

As I watched this morning, the familiar world outside my apartment window began to return. Trees emerged and the lake reappeared. The service road was still there, as was the bike path. The long grasses waved gently in the breeze. The fog rolled quietly away and disappeared. The houses were still standing, protecting their families that I didn't know but cherished. I was sure the woman in her bright outfit would soon appear on the service road, cross the connecting path, and walk briskly up the bike path.

The real world is not so real sometimes. It appears solid and unchanging, but that is part of its charm and mystique. Family members are with us for a while, and then they are swallowed up in the fog of the unknown and the unfamiliar. Our minds play tricks on us. Words we know so well disappear, and our best efforts fail to retrieve them. Memories of past events become cloudy, and we're not sure whether they really happened or whether we imagined them. Reality or illusion? Is there a difference?

Philosophers deal with questions such as, "What do we know, and how do we know it?" With a shrug, we say, "What difference does it make?" We know that what seems permanent today may be totally different tomorrow. We also know that some values we have lived by are real and unchanging. We are to love the Lord and our neighbors as ourselves, treat people with kindness, count our blessings, and always express our gratitude for this life and all we experience.

Many things disappear in the fog of time—our houses, our cherished belongings, our memories, even our beloved family members. The fog is soft and gentle, obscuring some things and revealing others. The fog will lift in time and the view will be wonderful, familiar, and yet new. Is there another world that will be revealed to us when we're ready? For now, all is well. Be at peace.

Personal Reflections on the Weekend

In January, I chose a weekend of ragtime music over a performance of the Des Moines Symphony Orchestra. It was an inspired choice I'll never regret. In addition to the music, the weekend included eagle viewing along the Mississippi River. It was a magical time of frigid, sunny days and brilliant, starry nights enclosing the exciting syncopation of ragtime music and the magnificent American bald eagles.

Both the human music and the soaring flights and dives of the eagles moved me. Both were joyous and yet sad; triumphs of survival as well as the eternal competition for the most basic needs. The music spoke of love and loss, of joy and sorrow. The eagles soared and roosted, fished for food, surveyed the water and land for nesting locations, and protected their domains. Seemingly solitary birds, the eagles mate for life, sharing the challenges and tedium of hatching, nurturing, and teaching their young.

The eagles regarded the visiting humans with indifference and a natural dignity. The visitors knew they were seeing magic on enormous wings.

We humans soar through our music, painting our joys and aspirations as well as plumbing the depths of our sorrows. The old beat of ragtime with its even older laments of hymns speak of the burdens humans carry. The music speaks of the longing for a power beyond understanding, of a reward somewhere, sometime, that cannot be seen but only hoped for. It is a promise for the faithful and forgiveness for the weak and sinful.

Sorrow comes to most of us along with brief times of joy. Ragtime expresses the reality of life for the burdened, the downtrodden, the poor, the underclasses. It speaks to those of color who have never really been free. It acknowledges the sorrow of their lives, but lightens their load with its driving tempo and message of hope. "Today is almost beyond enduring," the music says, "but tomorrow you will get your reward. We are weak, but He is strong. Oh yes, Lord."

We humans need music as much as eagles need flight. Where else should the comfort, excitement, and solace of ragtime, marches, jazz, and hymns be experienced more deeply than in a small Iowa church on a cold, brilliant weekend?

"I sing because I'm happy. I sing because I'm free."

"His eye is on the sparrow and I know He cares for me. Oh yes, Lord."

The lowly ragtime, a quintessential American music of the people, along with the American bald eagle, symbol of this country, defines us and touches our souls.

Dear Loving God,

We come to You this evening with relief. We have had a busy day and we need the reassurance of Your presence. Help us to be open to Your guidance, Your support, and Your love. Sometimes our lives are too hectic, too filled with busyness without meaning or joy. Your lessons guide us if we hear them and follow Your teachings.

In a dangerous and tragic world, You are our way to safety and peace. You give us hope when we feel hopeless. You remind us of eternal truths when we have lost our vision.

We pray for ourselves, our families, and our world. We pray for those who are suffering and who feel lost and alone. Be with us all and surround us with Your love. We are grateful for Your eternal presence in our lives. Be with us and among us. We long to be Your own.

Amen.

www.ingramcontent.com/pod-product-compliance
Lightning Source LLC
Chambersburg PA
CBHW031317040426
42443CB00005B/105